Corporate Sponsorship of Small-Scale Sport Tourism Events

Matthew Lamont

Corporate Sponsorship of Small-Scale Sport Tourism Events

An Australian Perspective

LAP LAMBERT Academic Publishing

Impressum/Imprint (nur für Deutschland/ only for Germany)
Bibliografische Information der Deutschen Nationalbibliothek: Die Deutsche Nationalbibliothek verzeichnet diese Publikation in der Deutschen Nationalbibliografie; detaillierte bibliografische Daten sind im Internet über http://dnb.d-nb.de abrufbar.

Alle in diesem Buch genannten Marken und Produktnamen unterliegen warenzeichen-, marken- oder patentrechtlichem Schutz bzw. sind Warenzeichen oder eingetragene Warenzeichen der jeweiligen Inhaber. Die Wiedergabe von Marken, Produktnamen, Gebrauchsnamen, Handelsnamen, Warenbezeichnungen u.s.w. in diesem Werk berechtigt auch ohne besondere Kennzeichnung nicht zu der Annahme, dass solche Namen im Sinne der Warenzeichen- und Markenschutzgesetzgebung als frei zu betrachten wären und daher von jedermann benutzt werden dürften.

Coverbild: www.ingimage.com

Verlag: LAP LAMBERT Academic Publishing AG & Co. KG
Dudweiler Landstr. 99, 66123 Saarbrücken, Deutschland
Telefon +49 681 3720-310, Telefax +49 681 3720-3109
Email: info@lap-publishing.com

Herstellung in Deutschland:
Schaltungsdienst Lange o.H.G., Berlin
Books on Demand GmbH, Norderstedt
Reha GmbH, Saarbrücken
Amazon Distribution GmbH, Leipzig
ISBN: 978-3-8383-1586-7

Imprint (only for USA, GB)
Bibliographic information published by the Deutsche Nationalbibliothek: The Deutsche Nationalbibliothek lists this publication in the Deutsche Nationalbibliografie; detailed bibliographic data are available in the Internet at http://dnb.d-nb.de.

Any brand names and product names mentioned in this book are subject to trademark, brand or patent protection and are trademarks or registered trademarks of their respective holders. The use of brand names, product names, common names, trade names, product descriptions etc. even without a particular marking in this works is in no way to be construed to mean that such names may be regarded as unrestricted in respect of trademark and brand protection legislation and could thus be used by anyone.

Cover image: www.ingimage.com

Publisher: LAP LAMBERT Academic Publishing AG & Co. KG
Dudweiler Landstr. 99, 66123 Saarbrücken, Germany
Phone +49 681 3720-310, Fax +49 681 3720-3109
Email: info@lap-publishing.com

Printed in the U.S.A.
Printed in the U.K. by (see last page)
ISBN: 978-3-8383-1586-7

Copyright © 2009 by the author and LAP LAMBERT Academic Publishing AG & Co. KG
and licensors
All rights reserved. Saarbrücken 2009

TABLE OF CONTENTS

Chapter One: Introduction 1
   1.1 Background to the Study 1
   1.2 Problem Statement 3
   1.3 Research Objectives 3
   1.4 Significance of the Study 4
   1.5 Overview of the Methodology 4
   1.6 Definitions of Terms 4
   1.7 Outline of the Work 5

Chapter Two: Literature Review 7
   2.1 Introduction 7
   2.2 Sponsorship Defined 7
   2.3 The Growth of Sport Sponsorship 10
   2.4 The Fit of Sponsorship into the Marketing Communications Mix 13
   2.5 Small and Medium Business Involvement in Sponsorship 16
   2.6 Special Events 18
   2.7 Sport Tourism Events 21
   2.8 Regional Sport Tourism Events 23
   2.9 Event Sponsorship 26
   2.10 Sponsorship of Sport Tourism Events 29
   2.11 Leveraging Event Sponsorships 31
   2.12 Evaluation of Sponsorship Effectiveness 33
   2.13 SME Sponsorship of Regional Sport Tourism Events 38
   2.14 Chapter Summary 41

Chapter Three: Methodology 42
   3.1 Introduction 42
   3.2 Research Paradigm 42
   3.3 Case Studies and Conditions for use of Case Studies 43
   3.4 Case Study Procedures 44
      3.4.1 Selection of cases 44
   3.5 Data Collection 49
      3.5.1 In-Depth Interviews 49
      3.5.2 Semi-Structured Interviews 50
   3.6 Data Analysis 52

3.7 Pilot Study 53
3.8 'Trustworthiness' of the Research 54
3.9 Chapter Summary 55
Chapter Four: Results 57
4.1 Introduction and Description of Cases 57
    4.1.1 Case Study Number One 57
    4.1.2 Case Study Number Two 58
    4.1.3 Case Study Number Three 58
    4.1.4 Case Study Number Four 59
    4.1.5 Case Study Number Five 60
4.2 In-Depth Interview Results 60
    4.2.1 Case Study One Results 61
    4.2.2 Case Study Two Results 64
    4.2.3 Case Study Three Results 67
    4.2.4 Case Study Four Results 70
    4.2.5 Case Study Five Results 72
4.3 Chapter Summary 76
Chapter Five: Discussion 77
5.1 Introduction 77
5.2 Sponsor & Event Manager Perceptions of Sponsorship 77
5.3 Reasons why Small and Medium Businesses Provided Sponsorship to
Regional Sport Tourism Events 80
5.4 Leveraging Practices in Small and Medium Business Sponsorships of
Regional Sport Tourism Events 83
5.5 Evaluation of Small and Medium Business Sponsorships of Regional
Sport Tourism Events 88
5.6 The Initiation of Sponsorship Agreements between Small and Medium
Businesses and Regional Sport Tourism Events 95
5.7 Process Model of Regional Sport Tourism Event Sponsorship by Small
and Medium Businesses 97
5.8 Chapter Summary 101
Chapter Six: Conclusion and Implications 102
6.1 Summary of the Study 102
6.2 Management Implications arising from this Research 104
6.3 Contribution to Knowledge 105

6.4 Limitations of the Research 106
6.5 Recommended Areas for Future Research 106
References 108
Appendices 117

CHAPTER ONE

INTRODUCTION

1.1 Background to the Study

Travel by human beings dates back to ancient times. Because of the nomadic patterns of our early ancestors, Leiper (1995) claimed that the phenomenon of tourism possesses a history as ancient as humans themselves. Today, tourism has evolved into one of the world's most significant industries. The World Travel and Tourism Council (2005) estimated that tourism would generate US$6.2 billion, account for 10.6% of Gross Domestic Product, and provide 221 million jobs worldwide during 2005.

Furthermore, special events, be they of a sporting, artistic or cultural nature, have evolved into a central component of contemporary life as well as a key sector of global tourism industries. The acceptance of special events by modern society has been attributed to factors such as increases in available leisure time and disposable income (Allen, O'Toole, McDonnell, & Harris, 2002). In particular, sporting events have provided a catalyst for tourism since as early as 900BC (Standeven & DeKnop, 1999) when the Greeks were observed travelling to watch and participate in the Ancient Greek Games, which have grown into the modern Olympic Games as we know them today.

The staging of small-scale sporting events that attract visitors has become increasingly popular with host communities (Dowell, 1999). Such events have the potential to generate a range of benefits to the host community such as a 'boost' to the local economy arising from visitor spending; smoothing out of 'troughs' in demand for tourist facilities such as restaurants, accommodation providers and attractions during periods of low business; and the potential to generate repeat visitation by event participants at other times of the year (Delpy, 1998).

However, the staging of successful sport tourism events is highly dependent upon the ability of event organisers to cover costs associated with running an event, such as marketing, infrastructure, staff and insurance. Revenue to cover such costs is often sourced from areas such as participation fees, merchandising, fundraising and sponsorship (Allen et al., 2002). Of these sources, sponsorship has frequently proven to be the source of revenue that provides the 'financial backbone' for many events. Sponsorship industry newsletter, the *IEG Sponsorship Report*, claimed that on average, 43% of any given event's revenue was comprised of sponsorship funds (IEG, 1992a). Sponsorship is often regarded as a key requirement for an event of any type to be successful. Furthermore, numerous authors agree that the sponsorship of sport tourism events are the most popular form of sponsorship investment for large corporate organisations (Delpy, 1998; Kuzma, Shanklin, & McCally, 1993; McDonald, 1991; Sunshine, Backman, & Backman, 1995).

Sponsorship has been described as a cash or in-kind investment by a commercial entity in an activity, such as a sporting event, for which it receives in exchange, access to exploitable features of the given property which may be used by the sponsor to obtain commercial advantage (Meenaghan, 1991). As with the tourism industry, sponsorship has matured into a large and constantly growing global industry, which was evidenced in 2002 when US$24.2 billion was spent on sponsorship of all causes by businesses worldwide (Kolah, 2003). Large businesses have discovered the potential for achieving their business objectives through sport sponsorship (Marshall & Cook, 1992; McCarville & Copeland, 1994; Stotlar, 2001). Objectives such as increasing awareness of an organisation; image enhancement; increasing sales; providing client hospitality; and motivating employees are common reasons cited by businesses in justifying why they engage in sport sponsorship (Stotlar, 2001).

Operational functions of sponsorship such as leveraging and evaluation have also attracted attention by the academic community. It has been suggested that in order to obtain maximum return from a sponsorship investment, it is insufficient to purchase a property alone (Abratt & Grobler, 1989; Pope & Voges, 1994). Numerous authorities in the sponsorship field felt that sponsorships should be *leveraged* (Crompton, 1993; Kinney & McDaniel, 1996; Meenaghan, 1991). 'Leveraging' refers to additional funds invested by the sponsor in complementary activities designed to properly exploit the sponsorship, such as advertising and in-store promotions.

Sponsorship is rarely perceived as a donation in today's business environment (Copeland, Frisby, & McCarville, 1996; Irwin & Asimakopoulos, 1992). Many sponsors now insist upon having their sponsorship investments justified by evaluating the effectiveness of such investments (Copeland et al., 1996). Measurements pertaining to factors such as the effects of a sponsorship investment on sales and communications objectives often form the basis for such evaluations (Marshall & Cook, 1992).

Authors such as Delpy, Grabijas and Stefanovich (1998) and Turco (1998) have stated that sport tourism events have proven to be the most popular form of sponsorship investment for the corporate world. At the regional level, sport tourism events are frequently underwritten by small and medium-sized businesses, often referred to as small and medium-sized enterprises (SMEs). However, little research has been carried out into why such businesses engage in such sponsorships (Slack & Bentz, 1996). Much of the scholarly literature addressing sponsorship and events has focused on large organisations and large sponsorships (Mack, 1999), and has tended to be quantitative in nature. There appears to be gaps in this literature pertaining to SME sponsorship of regional sport tourism events, which this research aims to address. Such gaps in knowledge include:

- Why SMEs sponsor regional sport tourism events;
- How event managers and sponsors in this context perceive sponsorship;
- If and how leveraging occurs in such sponsorship agreements;
- If and how evaluation takes place within these sponsorships; and
- How such agreements are initiated and the degree of formality involved.

Given the increasing importance placed on sport tourism events by regional areas for economic development, research is necessary to develop the body of knowledge pertaining to sponsorship of regional sport tourism events by SMEs. Development of this body of knowledge is also required to facilitate the successful staging of regional sport tourism events. This research will attempt to contribute to this body of knowledge by investigating the five literature gaps previously identified.

1.2 Problem Statement

This aim of this research to examine and explore managerial aspects of sponsorship agreements between small to medium-sized enterprises (SMEs) and regional sport tourism events in Northern New South Wales, Australia.

1.3 Research Objectives

The general aims of this research can be expressed more specifically by the following four research objectives:

1. Identify sponsors' and event managers' perceptions as to what constitutes 'sponsorship';
2. Identify the reasons why small and medium businesses provide sponsorship to regional sport tourism events;
3. Explore if and how leveraging is conducted within small and medium business/regional sport tourism event sponsorships;
4. Explore if and how event managers and sponsors evaluated the effectiveness of their sponsorship agreement; and
5. Examine how sponsorship agreements between small and medium businesses were initiated with regional sport tourism events.

1.4 Significance of the Study

SMEs extensively provide cash or in-kind sponsorship to sport events at the regional level. In many cases sponsorship revenues obtained from SMEs is the financial lifeblood of these small-scale events. However, little research has been conducted into such agreements to date. A better understanding of *why* SMEs are motivated to provide sponsorship to regional sport tourism events may enable event managers to more effectively attract and maintain sponsorship funds for their events. Further, examination of operational functions of sponsorships (namely leveraging and evaluation) may result in highlighting a need for training materials and/or courses for persons involved in the managing the sponsorships of regional sport tourism events.

This research responds to calls by Turco (1998) and Arthur (1999) for further research into sport tourism sponsorship and small business sponsorship. Turco (1998) felt that given the growth of both sponsorship and the sport tourism industry, analysis of sponsorships within this phenomenon was warranted. Meanwhile, Arthur (1999) has called for research into the sponsorship practices of small businesses. He felt that there was growing evidence to suggest that sport at a lower level (meaning sport other than at a professional level) than that examined in his research, is dependent upon sponsorship funds.

1.5 Overview of the Methodology

In order to satisfy the research objectives of this research, a qualitative case study research strategy was chosen in order to elicit deep, rich data from the research participants. Five regional sport tourism events were purposively selected from the research area, which formed the basis of five case studies. Semi-structured interviews were conducted with five managers of regional sport tourism events, in addition to interviewing the owner or manager of one sponsoring business of each event. Collected data was then analysed utilising a three-stage process of qualitative data analysis proposed by Miles and Huberman (1994). A comprehensive description and justification for this research approach is provided in Chapter Three.

1.6 Definitions of Terms

Large business: Businesses employing 200 or more people (Australian Bureau of Statistics, 2001).

Medium business: 'Businesses employing twenty or more people, but less than 200 people' (Australian Bureau of Statistics, 2001, p. 123).

Northern New South Wales: An area defined by the researcher as a geographical area extending from the New South Wales/Queensland border, south to Coffs Harbour, and inland as far as Casino.

Regional: Those parts of Australia distant from the major international ports of entry (Centre for Regional Tourism Research, 2001).

Regional sport tourism event: Sports activities held on an infrequent basis, conducted in areas distant from major international ports of entry that attract a sizeable number of visiting participants and/or spectators to the host community. Such events also have the potential to attract non-resident media, technical personnel and other sports officials (adapted from Delpy, 1998).

Small business: 'Businesses employing less than twenty people in all industries except agriculture where the definition is businesses with an EVAO [estimated value of agricultural operations] of between $22,500 and $400,000' (Australian Bureau of Statistics, 2001, p. 124).

SME: Small and medium-sized enterprise. A business which employs between one and two hundred persons.

Sponsorship: 'The provision of resources (e.g. money, people, equipment) by an organisation directly to an event or activity in exchange for a direct association to the event or activity. The providing organisation can then use this direct association to achieve either their corporate, marketing or media objectives' (Sandler & Shani, 1989, p. 10).

Sport tourism: 'All forms of active and passive involvement in sporting activity, participated in casually or in an organised way for non-commercial or business/commercial reasons, that necessitate travel away from home and work locality' (Standeven & DeKnop, 1999, p. 12).

Sport tourism event: 'Sports activities that attract a sizeable number of visiting participants and/or spectators … with the potential to attract non-resident media and technical personnel and other sports officials' (Delpy, 1998, p. 31).

1.7 Outline of the Work

Following on from this introductory chapter, Chapter Two presents the review of literature related to this research. Sponsorship is first defined, followed by an analysis of its history and growth into a large global industry. SMEs are then described, in addition to their involvement in sponsorship. The chapter then goes on to present the literature pertaining to special events and event sponsorship, with special reference to sport tourism events. Operational functions of sponsorship, namely leveraging and evaluation are then presented, before reviewing the literature specifically examining this research topic, which is SME sponsorship of regional sport tourism events.

Chapter Three contains a comprehensive overview of, and justification for the use of the methodological processes employed to conduct this research. The chapter initially justifies the selection of an interpretive paradigm to guide the research and the use of a case study research approach. The procedure for selecting events and sponsors for inclusion in the research is then outlined, along with the method of data collection. Finally, the chapter presents the delimitations, data analysis procedures, description of the pilot study, and then concludes with how trustworthiness of the research was established.

The results of in-depth interviews with event managers and sponsors are presented in Chapter Four. Background information for each case study is provided in the early sections of the chapter, before the results of each case are presented individually. Results are presented utilising the five research objectives of this study as subheadings within each individual case.

Chapter Five contains a detailed discussion of the results presented Chapter Four. The findings are discussed in light of the literature presented in Chapter Two, in addition to proposing a range of original concepts, including a process model of SME sponsorship of regional sport tourism events, which emerged during the compilation of Chapter Five. The chapter is divided into five main sections, with the discussion presented utilising this study's five research objectives as points of discussion.

Chapter Six provides the conclusion to this work. The chapter summarises the findings of this research and goes on to outline the managerial implications arising from this study. The contribution to the body of knowledge regarding SME sponsorship of regional sport tourism events made by this study is then described. Finally, the limitations surrounding this research are outlined and acknowledged, and several areas for future research are identified.

CHAPTER TWO

LITERATURE REVIEW

2.1 Introduction

The nature of this research topic encompasses a wide range of subject areas that have attracted attention within the academic literature. Sections 2.2 through 2.4 address definitions of sponsorship, the history and growth of sponsorship and sponsorship's role in the marketing communications mix, while Section 2.5 explores SME sponsorship usage. Sections 2.6 to 2.8 investigate special events, sport tourism events and regional sport tourism events. Section 2.9 onwards address themes specific to this research, which include event sponsorship, sponsorship leveraging, sponsorship evaluation, and finally the sponsorship of regional sport tourism events by SMEs.

2.2 Sponsorship Defined

Many attempts have been made at defining the term 'sponsorship', however to date no one explanation is accepted as the unanimously authoritative definition. Sleight (1989), in referring to the broad opinions on the subject, went as far as describing sponsorship as 'three syllables that form what must be one of the most abused and misunderstood words in the English language' (p. 3). A selection of definitions proposed by various researchers within the literature included those of Sleight (1989), Meenaghan (1991), and Scott and Suchard (1992), which stated:

> Sponsorship is a business relationship between a provider of funds, resources or services and an individual, event or organisation which offers in return some rights and association that may be used for commercial advantage (Sleight, 1989, p. 4).

> Commercial sponsorship is an investment, in cash or in kind, in an activity, in return for access to the exploitable commercial potential associated with that activity (Meenaghan, 1991, p. 10).

> A significant, finite, prior commitment to underwriting part or all of the costs of staging an event or series of events (cash or in-kind) in return for an acknowledgement by the sponsored body of the sponsor's underwriting of the event(s) (Scott & Suchard, 1992, p. 11).

The three cited definitions describe sponsorship as being an exchange of resources between two parties, capable of yielding mutual benefit. Such a relationship was viewed by McCarville and Copeland (1994) as an 'exchange relationship', because sponsorship involves an exchange of resources (such as cash, product, or labour) with an independent partner, with the aim of gaining a return on the investment:

> Sponsorship involves an exchange of resources with an independent partner in hope of gaining a corresponding return from the sponsor. The notion of mutual return distinguishes sponsorship from other forms of corporate support like philanthropy, charity and patronage, which do not involve the advancement of commercial objectives. Sponsorship is undertaken so that both partners can benefit (p. 103).

Authors such as Stotlar (2001) and Crompton (1994) shared McCarville and Copeland's view of sponsorship as an exchange relationship. In fact Stotlar (2001) suggested that sponsorship can be viewed as a symbiotic relationship, owing to the two involved parties' reliance on simultaneously providing and receiving benefits from one-another.

Molm (1990) felt that in order for an exchange relationship in a commercial sponsorship context to exist, two pre-existing conditions must be in place. They were a) at least two parties must exchange some form of resources, be they physical, financial, or intangible (such as status, approval, or expertise); and b) the exchanged resources must be of value to the reciprocating party (p. 428).

Mullin, Hardy and Sutton (1993) contributed some conjecture to the meaning of sponsorship, by associating sponsorship with *promotional licencing*. These authors claimed that the term *sponsorship* was often used to describe activities such as 'Blockbuster Video obtaining the rights to all major league videocassettes' (p. 204), is somewhat misleading. Mullin et al. felt that situations such as this were actually a form of promotional licencing. These authors gave a further example of promotional licencing as 'the right to use a logo, a name, a trademark, and graphic representation signifying the purchasers' connection with the product/event. These rights can be used in advertising, promotion, publicity, or other communication activities employed by the purchaser' (p. 204). Drawing from this example, it seems these authors were suggesting that sponsorship and promotional licencing are terms that can be used interchangeably. Lee, Sandler and Shani (1997) felt that Mullin et al.'s suggestion that sponsorship was also promotional licencing did little more than to add confusion to the issue. In a further contribution to a definition of sponsorship, Meenaghan (2001) wrote that commercial sponsorship is 'also known as lifestyle, event, and sports marketing' (p. 191), adding even more diversity to the meaning of the term.

According to Speed and Thompson (2000), sponsorship is dissimilar to advertising, owing to the involvement of a second party, which is the activity or cause sponsored. However, Abratt and Grobler (1989) disagreed with Speed and Thompson. Abratt and Grobler claimed that sponsorship *is* a form of advertising, as sponsoring businesses strategically place their brand names on the sponsored property (for example on the jerseys of football teams and perimeter signage at stadiums).

Interestingly, none of the definitions cited explicitly stated that sponsorship is distinctly different from *charity* or *philanthropy*, despite this being a highly concurrent view within the reviewed literature (Copeland et al., 1996; Head, 1988; Irwin & Asimakopoulos, 1992). Amis, Pant and Slack (1997) reinforced this view in suggesting that large firms such as petroleum giant Mobil, are unlikely to enter into a sponsorship without strong evidence that such an investment will result in a distinct competitive advantage for the business.

Philanthropy differs from commercial sponsorship in that philanthropy involves a donation, from which expectation of a commercial reward is *not* expected by the donor (Bennett, 1997). In contrast, sponsorship *does* involve an expectation on the donor's behalf of some sort of commercial return. Crompton (1997) felt that the terms 'sponsorship' and 'donation' are often used 'interchangeably and are considered to be synonymous' (p. 39), and that voluntary exchange is also inherit amongst the two. However, Crompton echoed Molm's (1990) view by stating that in order for an arrangement to constitute 'sponsorship', both parties must offer one-another something of value.

Research by Copeland et al. (1996) surveyed seventy-five Canadian corporations with advertising budgets in excess of CAD$50,000 and who were involved in sport sponsorship, established that none of their respondents perceived their sport sponsorship investments as philanthropy. All respondents indicated that their sport sponsorship involvement was inextricably linked to their businesses' 'bottom-line' and increasing sales through targeting specific market segments. Similarly, investigation by Stotlar (1999) concluded that the data he gathered supported a contention that 'sponsorship is clearly and rapidly moving away from rationale based on social responsibility and obscure conceptions of image enhancement to more purely definable business motives' (p. 98). Brown (2002) noted that Ansett Airlines sought to generate AU$200 million in new business from their sponsorship of the 2000 Sydney Olympic Games, which provided an example of bottom-line objectives businesses seek to achieve through sponsorship.

In advancing sponsorship's distinction between other forms of commercial promotional activity, Otker (1988) differentiated sponsorship from advertising by affirming that sponsorship is an activity centred outside a company's main operations, 'it [sponsorship] is a business agreement built up on the basis of an event, a team, a personality, and/or an organisation which will, it is hoped, benefit both the sponsor and the sponsored body' (p. 77). Advertising, on the other hand was considered to be a component of a company's core marketing communication elements.

Sponsorship may take the form of a cash payment, or provision of in-kind products or services to an individual, cause or event (Allen et al., 2002). The term *in-kind* sponsorship is often used interchangeably with the term *contra* sponsorship (Geldard & Sinclair, 1996). The provision of in-kind sponsorship can be defined as 'the payment of some or all of the fee in products and/or services in lieu of cash' (Geldard & Sinclair, 1996, p. 153). Thus an example of in-kind sponsorship would be that of a waste collection company providing waste collection services to a sports event free of charge, in exchange for signage or advertising opportunities at that event.

For the purpose of this research which examines sport tourism events, sponsorship shall be defined according to the definition proposed by Sandler and Shani (1989). These authors defined sponsorship as:

> The provision of resources (e.g. money, people, equipment) by an organisation directly to an event or activity in exchange for a direct association to the event or activity. The providing organisation can then use this direct association to achieve either their corporate, marketing or media objectives (p. 10).

The definition of Sandler and Shani (1989) was adopted firstly as it pertained specifically to an event, which is pertinent to the present study. Additionally, this definition was chosen as it offered some explanation as to why businesses desire association with an event or activity through sponsorship, which was to achieve corporate, marketing or media objectives, whereas the previously cited definitions failed to do so.

Section 2.2 established that sponsorship is a reciprocal business exchange of resources between two parties, which is capable of yielding mutual benefits for all involved. Sponsorship was clearly distinct from advertising in that it was often used as a strategic tool to reach specific market segments, and is dissimilar to philanthropy in that the sponsoring party expects a commercial return on its investment. Given that this research aims to investigate the sponsorship of regional sport tourism events by SMEs, it was necessary to develop an understanding of the factors that constitute sponsorship in addition to setting boundaries regarding the meaning of the term. Section 2.3 now reviews the literature examining the evolution of sport sponsorship.

2.3 The Growth of Sport Sponsorship

According to Skinner and Rukavina (2003), sport sponsorship has evolved along the course of seven distinct stages. Stage One occurred during the period 1 B.C. to 1600, and was dubbed the 'Era of Patronage'. Sponsorship occurred in the form of wealthy individuals (as opposed to businesses) sponsoring high-profile artists such as Michelangelo and Leonardo Da Vinci. However, there was some conjecture in the literature as to when the first occurrence of sport sponsorship actually took place; Head (1988) claimed that sponsorship of sport was first observed back in the days of Caesar, approximately 65 B.C. when he sponsored gladiatorial festivals for the purpose of increasing his esteem. Further, Turner (2001) felt that the first form of sponsorship *per se* occurred in 1492 when Queen Isabella of Spain funded Christopher Columbus' venture to discover the Americas.

The year 1631 saw the 'Advent of Advertising' when businesses realised the potential for exposure through advertising in print media. The 'Early Pioneers' was an era occurring between 1924 and 1970 during which cigarette, alcohol and automobile companies began lending their name to high-profile events such as the Indianapolis 500 motor race.

During the period 1970-1984, many companies realised they could obtain 'free' television exposure for their brand through sponsoring high-profile sporting events; this era was hailed as the 'Era of Development'. At this point in time, sponsors were content to be offered signage and hospitality opportunities. Owing to a shortfall in government funding for the 1984 Los Angeles Olympic Games, US$400 million of sponsorship was sold off in 1983, which sparked 'The Sponsorship Explosion'. It was at this time that 'companies found that they could increase sales through sponsorship' (Skinner & Rukavina, 2003, p. xx). Sponsors became more sophisticated during the 'Era of Added Value' that occurred during the 1990's; measured results and justification for investment became increasingly important. Owing to the advances in technology (primarily the development of the Internet) sponsorship occurs today in what is termed the 'Technological Era'.

Sponsorship of all causes (i.e. sport, the arts, festivals, attractions and the like) has matured into a significant global industry (IEG, 2003). Sponsorship spending has also shown a steady growth in recent years in comparison to other promotional activities such as advertising and sales promotion. Industry publication, the *IEG Sponsorship Report* predicted that worldwide sponsorship expenditure would total US$28 billion in 2004, which represented an 8.1% increase from US$25.9 billion in 2003 (IEG, 2003), which demonstrated sponsorship's increasing popularity in the corporate world.

Sponsorship has become immensely popular amongst corporate society in its endeavours to achieve business objectives, and as part of the marketing/communications mix (Javalgi, Traylor, Gross, & Lampman, 1994; Meenaghan, 1991). Corporate organisations are inundated with requests for sponsorship each year. Many organisations are forced to employ staff specifically to deal with incoming sponsorship proposals and the selection of appropriate sponsorship opportunities (Arthur, Scott, & Woods, 1997; Kuzma et al., 1993; Morris & Irwin, 1996).

Research into sponsorship activities by Australian businesses by Suchard and Scott (1992) commented that, 'sponsorship in Australia plays a relatively minor role in the overall promotional mix, which is dominated by television, magazine and newspaper advertising' (p. 25). These authors quoted an average spend of between AU$400,000 and AU$600,000 (per business) annually on sponsorship of all causes for the sample surveyed, and stated that sponsorship appeared to be growing in usage. It was reported that during 1996-97, 38 900 businesses (6.4% of all businesses in Australia) provided sponsorship to individuals or organisations, with the most popular form of investment being sport sponsorship (Australian Bureau of Statistics, 1999). The total value of sponsorship expenditure for this period was AU$466.5 million, with AU$281.9 million being spent on sport sponsorship (Australian Bureau of Statistics, 1999), which served to illustrate the popularity of sport sponsorship amongst Australian businesses.

Meenaghan (1991) has identified six driving forces which he felt have contributed to the exponential growth of sport sponsorship. They were:

1. Changing government policies on tobacco advertising;
2. The rising cost of traditional advertising media;
3. Sponsorship's proven ability in achieving marketing objectives;
4. New sponsorship opportunities arising from society's increasing time devoted to leisure;
5. Increased media coverage of sponsored events; and
6. Inefficiencies associated with traditional media.

Otker (1988) offered similar views to those stated by Meenaghan (1991) in explaining sponsorship's rapid growth, particularly in relation to the prohibitive costs of media advertising, and society's increasing leisure time. Otker claimed that the growth of traditional and new forms of media were in need of more attractive programming, and that such attractive programming could often be found in the sporting and cultural arena. Further explanation proposed by Otker included event organising bodies looking for new sources to finance their events; the media looking for new events to pay attention to; companies looking for new means to communicate with their target markets; and finally, the emergence of professional intermediaries whom specialise in managing sponsorships.

Section 2.3 found that sponsorship first occurred as early as 1 B.C. and has evolved along the course of seven stages. Over time sponsorship has shifted from a philanthropic practice to one inextricably linked to the bottom-line. Today, businesses worldwide allocate significant amounts of money to sponsorship, which has resulted in sponsorship emerging into a significant global industry. Researchers such as Meenaghan (1991) and Otker (1988) offered explanations as to why sponsorship has grown in popularity. It was important to discuss the evolution of sponsorship, as it contributes to understanding why businesses so frequently engage in sponsorship today, which is linked to the second research objective of the present study – to identify the reasons why SMEs sponsor regional sport tourism events. Section 2.4 now reviews the literature investigating sponsorship's place in the marketing communications mix.

2.4 The Fit of Sponsorship into the Marketing Communications Mix

Businesses have a need to communicate with their publics. According to Sleight (1989), 'in every aspect of corporate life the need to communicate a range of messages to a variety of different audiences is of paramount importance' (p. 29). Audiences which businesses have a need to communicate with include the general public, the media, company employees, shareholders and suppliers (Meenaghan, 1991). As sponsorship has grown in popularity during recent decades, so has its acceptance as an integral part of the marketing communications mix. Sleight (1989) felt that the underlying reason why businesses engage in sponsorship was to assist with fulfilling their communication needs.

The marketing communications mix, or 'marketing mix' consists of four variables: product, price, promotion and place, which a business is able to manipulate in order to achieve its marketing objectives. These four variables are collectively known as the 'four P's' of marketing (Kotler, Brown, Adam, & Armstrong, 2001). There was a general concurrence within the literature that sponsorship falls under the umbrella of *promotion* within the marketing mix alongside advertising, personal selling, publicity and sales promotions (Allen et al., 2002; Meenaghan, 1991; Mullin et al., 1993; Sleight, 1989). Meenaghan (1991) felt that sponsorship fitted neatly into this category because its basic function 'lies in achieving marketing communications objectives' (p. 39).

Several studies have investigated why businesses engage in sponsorship, whether it be sponsorship of sport or any other cause. Examples of such work included, Quinn (1982), Abratt, Clayton and Pitt (1987), Scott and Suchard (1992), Arthur (1999), Stotlar (1999) and Carter and Wilkinson (2000). Quinn (1982) undertook one of the first examinations into the reasons why companies entered into sponsorship agreements. It was found that the most prevalent reasons why businesses engaged in sponsorship were in reaction to requests for sponsorship from organisations and individuals, followed by developing and maintaining their corporate image. The outcomes of Quinn's research are summarised in Table 2.1.

Abratt et al. (1987) investigated why businesses utilised sport sponsorship as part of their communications strategy. Forty-five South African businesses that had received media exposure during the period November 1984 to March 1985 were quantitatively surveyed. It was found that television coverage as a result of sponsorship was the most important reason driving the surveyed businesses to engage in sport sponsorship. Second and third most important were 'promoting corporate image', and 'potential media coverage' via print media and radio, respectively.

Table 2.1: Reasons for entering into sponsorship (source: Quinn, 1982, p. 312).

Reasons for Sponsorship	%
In response to requests from organisations/individuals	25.0
To develop/maintain the corporate image	20.8
To give a return to the community	12.5
To gain publicity for the company/products	12.5
To be seen as benevolent	8.3
To reflect the interests of management	8.3
To go across the full spectrum of media activities	4.2
To get feedback from customers	4.2

During their study into motivations for sponsorship expenditure by Australian businesses with an advertising budget of AU$50,000 or more, Scott and Suchard (1992) found two factors: 'performance' and 'client relationships' to be significantly related to the proportion of expenditure on sponsorship. In this case, 'performance' encompassed improving company/product awareness and market share, and 'client relationships' pertained to opportunities to provide client/guest hospitality. Scott and Suchard's results indicated that media coverage did not have any influence on promotional managers' decisions to allocate sponsorship funding. It should be noted that Scott and Suchard's research took place during the 'era of added value' proposed by Skinner and Rukavina (2003), which validated these authors' claim that sponsors became more sophisticated and interested in increasing sales through sponsorship at that point in time.

Arthur (1999) examined the corporate decision making process of sport sponsorship in Australia, in which sixty-one 'major' sponsors of sport in Australia were quantitatively surveyed regarding many aspects of their involvement in sport sponsorship. Results from this research found that increased brand awareness, increased company awareness and brand positioning were the most frequent objectives cited by businesses when embarking on a sport sponsorship program. Arthur's findings echoed those of Scott and Suchard (1992) in that brand and company awareness were amongst the most frequently cited reasons for engaging in sponsorship. Further substantiating Scott and Suchard's finding that media coverage was not on the very top of the list of sponsorship objectives, this factor was ranked as the fifth most important objective in a sponsorship program by Australian businesses (Arthur, 1999).

Stotlar (1999) reported that the ability to create new customers; increase sales; availability of hospitality opportunities; and tie-ins to current theme/marketing strategy were amongst the most important sponsorship objectives of North American sports executives. Stotlar's research surveyed twenty-four of the most active North American companies involved in sponsorship. Stotlar's finding of 'ability to create new customers' as the most popular response was exceptionally different to Arthur's (1999) discovery of 'increased brand awareness', which highlighted a difficulty with inferring the results of each study of this nature to the wider population.

Carter and Wilkinson (2000) conducted an investigation into reasons why companies provided sponsorship to the Sydney 2000 Olympic Games. This research quantitatively surveyed twenty-five firms named by SOCOG (Sydney Organising Committee for the Olympic Games) as providing sponsorship to the Games. Carter and Wilkinson's results ranked the following reasons for businesses providing sponsorship to the 2000 Olympic Games, in order of importance:

1. Increasing employee morale;
2. Showcasing a product or product line;
3. Reaching specific audiences;
4. Enhancing community image;
5. Increasing brand awareness; and
6. Increasing profits (source: Carter & Wilkinson, 2000, p. 177).

Carter and Wilkinson's results contradicted those of Arthur (1999) and Scott and Suchard (1992), in that performance-based objectives such as brand awareness and increased profits were found to be of less importance. Meanwhile, Brown (2000) offered somewhat contrasting views to Carter and Wilkinson regarding the objectives of major Sydney 2000 Olympic Games sponsors. Brown found that AMP Insurance, Ansett Airlines and VISA sponsored the Games explicitly to increase market share, 'return on investment is a critical concern, with commercial outcomes regarded as the most important objectives' (p. 86).

Section 2.4 established that sponsorship is today an accepted vehicle for businesses to communicate with their publics and achieve their objectives. Numerous studies have investigated why businesses engage in sponsorship. As a result, a body of knowledge has emerged which indicates that businesses engage in sponsorship for many reasons. These include the need to increase sales, to motivate employees, be seen as a good corporate citizen, and to increase brand awareness. A review of such previous studies was integral in conducting this research, as one objective of this study was to identify the reasons why small and medium businesses provide sponsorship to regional sport tourism events. As such, Section 2.5 now reviews the literature regarding the involvement of small and medium businesses in sponsorship.

2.5 Small and Medium Business Involvement in Sponsorship

Small businesses have been described as 'businesses employing less than twenty people in all industries except agriculture where the definition is businesses with an EVAO [estimated value of agricultural operations] of between $22,500 and $400,000' (Australian Bureau of Statistics, 2001, p. 124), and medium businesses as 'businesses employing twenty or more people but less than 200' (Australian Bureau of Statistics, 2001, p. 123). Of the 612,300 businesses operating in Australia during the period 1996-1997, 583,300 were small businesses and 26,700 were medium businesses (Australian Bureau of Statistics, 1999). Typically, such businesses exhibit characteristics such as independent ownership and operations; close control by owners/managers who also contributed most, if not, all the operating capital; and principal decision-making made by the owners/managers (Australian Bureau of Statistics, 2001). Collectively, small and medium businesses are known as SMEs (small and medium-sized enterprises) (Parker, 2000).

Gardner and Shuman (1988) detected a trend that smaller firms were discovering that sponsorships could be a 'cost-effective way to achieve their communication goals' (p. 44). In identifying this trend, Gardner and Shuman suggested a number of explanations as to why small businesses were becoming interested in sponsorship:

a) **Large companies dominating the advertising channels**

Sponsorship offers small businesses with relatively small communications budgets the opportunity to reach their publics in a significantly cheaper manner than purchasing advertising. Additionally, sponsorship allows small businesses to overcome media 'clutter' and inefficiencies associated with traditional media such as channel surfing, or *zapping* as Meenaghan (1991) referred to in his work.

b) **In order to target narrow, hard-to-reach audiences**

Sponsorships provide small businesses with a viable alternative to advertising by sponsoring causes associated with specific target markets. The wealthy for example; a small business may target this niche market by sponsoring chess tournaments as chess tournaments are known for attracting a participant base with a typically wealthy demographic.

c) When product demonstration is critical

Gardner and Shuman (1988) claimed, 'sometimes the direct experiences provided by sponsorships communicate more effectively than the indirect experiences provided by advertising' (p. 48). Given that consumers *choose* to attend events they are more likely to be receptive to a sponsors' message, as opposed to advertising which they are involuntarily exposed to. This view was shared by Brooks (1994), who felt that when people attend events, their 'guard is down' (p. 167) and they are more receptive to receive product messages. Gardner and Shuman stated that small businesses are able to take advantage of the active nature of sponsorships and provide prospective customers with direct product trial experiences.

In Australia, the contribution by SMEs to sponsorship of all causes is significant. Research by the Australian Bureau of Statistics (1999) valued the combined contribution of small and medium business sponsorship at AU$194.3 million dollars during the 1996/97 financial year. By far the most popular cause to allocate sponsorship funds by all categories of business, was sport.

Slack and Bentz (1996) agreed with Gardner and Shuman (1988) that small and medium businesses are extensively involved in sponsorship by proposing that,

> Even the most casual observer cannot fail to note the extent to which these type of organisations are involved in community youth and recreational sport. Team uniforms, programs, trophies and award banquets are often, in whole or in part, underwritten by local businesses such as restaurants, petrol stations, or car dealerships (Slack & Bentz, 1996, p. 175).

To date, little research has been carried out into SME involvement in sponsorship of all causes, let-alone sport sponsorship. Despite concurrence within the literature that SMEs are extensively involved in sponsorship, concurrence also exists in a view that small and medium business sponsorship has been neglected by the academic community, and that research into sponsorship has primarily focused on 'big' business. Mack (1999) stated that 'the majority of this literature tends to focus on large organisations and large sponsorships' (p. 26); while Gardner and Shuman (1998) wrote, 'in spite of the presence and growing importance of sponsorships, little research has been conducted in this area' (p. 44).

Mack (1999) conducted research into small business objectives, practices and perceptions with regard to sponsorship of events, which involved a two-stage methodology. Initially, qualitative focus group interviews with small business owners with the aim of utilising the outcomes to formulate a quantitative questionnaire for use in the second stage. Results from the first phase of the research revealed that community support; employee involvement; and reaching target markets were the primary objectives in place for engaging in event sponsorship by the participants. It was found that marketing objectives were of secondary importance.

The quantitative phase of Mack's (1999) research surveyed 212 American small businesses. Outcomes of the quantitative study echoed the results of Mack's first-stage qualitative inquiry, which found that community-based rationales motivated small businesses to provide sponsorship to events. 'Giving back to community' and 'interest and concern about event' ranked amongst the top three reasons for providing sponsorship. When quizzed on their opinions of sponsorship, 'sponsorship provides community assistance' was the most concurrently viewed statement amongst the respondents, again reinforcing the community involvement theme that Mack's research ascertained. Additionally, Mack (1999) found that family-run businesses were more likely to sponsor health-related events. Also, 80% of respondents stated that they sponsored the same events on a continuous basis.

Section 2.5 has shown that sponsorship provides small businesses with a cost-effective means of communicating their marketing messages to their publics. Sponsorship allows small businesses to communicate with hard to reach market segments and overcome inefficiencies associated with traditional advertising methods. Previous research also suggested that such businesses engaged in sponsorship for community purposes, and that small businesses see sponsorship as a means of giving back to their community. This study aims to examine SME sponsorship of regional sport tourism events, consequently, an examination of the literature pertaining to the sponsorship activities of SMEs was necessary to establish what is current knowledge about such a phenomenon. Section 2.6 now presents the literature examining research into special events.

2.6 Special Events

It has been suggested by Allen et al, (2002) that factors such as modern society's increasing time that can be devoted to leisure, coupled with an increase in discretionary spending have caused special events to become central to our culture. Governments encourage and financially support the use of special events in economic development, while businesses embrace special events as part of their marketing strategies (Allen et al., 2002). Jago and Shaw (1998) stated that the number of special events on regional event calendars has grown substantially in recent years, primarily attributed to the ability of special events to raise the profile of the host region via the extensive media coverage such events are capable of generating. Getz (1991) offered his definition by stating;

> A special event is a onetime or infrequently occurring event outside the normal program or activities of the sponsoring or organising body. To the customer, a special event is an opportunity for a leisure, social, or cultural experience outside the normal range of choices or beyond everyday experience (p. 44).

Jago and Shaw (1998) suggested that owing to the vast range of types of special events 'it is unlikely that a single, all-embracing definition of special events can be developed' (p. 29). However, in contributing to the body of knowledge attempting to define special events, Jago and Shaw's research identified a number of 'core attributes' that a phenomenon must meet before it can be accepted as a special event. Based on their findings, the core attributes of special events were suggested to be:

1. Attracting tourists or tourism development;
2. Being of a limited duration;
3. Being a one-off or infrequent occurrence;
4. Raising the awareness, image, or profile of a region;
5. Offering a social experience; and
6. Being out of the ordinary (Jago & Shaw, 1998, p. 29).

Events may be categorised according to their scale of impacts, which can include attendance numbers, media profile, infrastructure, costs and benefits (Allen et al., 2002). Categories which events can be segregated into include mega-events, hallmark events, major events, and local events (Getz, 1997).

In describing the different typologies of events, *mega-events* were depicted as events so large that 'they affect whole economies and reverberate in the global media' (Allen et al., 2002, p. 12), for example, the Olympic Games and World Fairs. Getz (1997) suggested that to be classed as a mega-event, attendance should exceed one million and capital costs should total at least US$500 million. Mega-events often provide a catalyst for the construction or expansion of additional tourism infrastructure in a host city, in addition to the refurbishment of existing infrastructure (Faulkner et al., 2001). However, it should be noted that on occasions, development legacies of mega-events can leave behind under-utilised and expensive facilities that ultimately accrue significant financial debt; the 1976 Montreal Olympic Games being a prime example (Higham, 1999). On the other hand, such events are also capable of attracting significant numbers of visitors to a host city. For example, the 2003 Rugby Union World Cup attracted 65,000 international visitors to Australia during the tournament, who spent on average AU$6,308 each during their stay (URS Finance and Economics, 2004).

Hallmark events are slightly smaller in scale to a mega-event, with the differentiating factor being that a hallmark event is synonymous with one city or region (Allen et al., 2002). Examples include the Kentucky Derby in the USA and the Tour De France cycle race. Getz (1997) described a hallmark event as 'a recurring event that possesses such significance, in terms of tradition, attractiveness, image, or publicity, that the event provides the host venue, community, or destination with a competitive advantage' (p. 5).

Major events, through their scale and media interest are capable of attracting significant visitor numbers, media coverage and economic benefits, however, not on the magnitude of mega or hallmark events (Allen et al., 2002). The Australian Open Tennis tournament and motor racing's Australian Formula One Grand Prix are examples of major events. Allen et al. also suggested that many top sporting events fit into this category. Due to the associated economic benefits associated with such events, fierce competition amongst countries exists in bidding for the right to host major sporting events.

The smallest scale events are termed *local events*. In a sporting context, such events are characterised by being run and organised by community sporting groups and making use of existing sport and tourism infrastructure (Walo, Bull, & Breen, 1996), as opposed to constructing infrastructure requirements specifically to aid in the staging of a mega event. Dowell (1999) agreed with Walo et al. in suggesting that smaller sport tourism events in regional areas are 'sustainable from economic, social and environmental perspectives' (p. 6) due to their use of existing infrastructure and low cost to the community.

Section 2.6 established that special events have progressed to become a central component of modern society. Governments provide support to many special events due to the benefits that host communities are able to accrue while corporations large and small have embraced special events owing to their ability to achieve corporate objectives. Special events can take place in a small town context or on a massive scale, which draws global attention. Each special event brings with it a portfolio of positive and negative social, economic, environmental, political and cultural impacts proportionate to an event's magnitude. As this research examines regional sport tourism events, it was essential to review this literature in order to define an 'event' and to establish where in the hierarchy of events, regional events fit. The literature pertaining to sport tourism events is now presented in Section 2.7.

2.7 Sport Tourism Events

The notion of travelling to participate in or to observe sport dates back to as early as 900BC when the Greeks were observed travelling to participate in and watch the Ancient Greek Games (Standeven & DeKnop, 1999). This phenomenon is termed *sport tourism*. However, academics have struggled to compose universally accepted definitions of sport and tourism in their own right and such difficulty has been attributed to the complex nature of sport and tourism, hence the lack of a universally accepted definition of sport tourism to date (Gibson, 1998). In terms of being recognised as an academic field of study, sport tourism has only been acknowledged in this regard since the late 1980's and early 1990's (Gibson, 1998). Today sport tourism is a significant and growing sector of the global tourism market, in addition to becoming a well-accepted academic field:

> Today vast numbers of people are interested in sport and almost everyone aspires to a holiday. Though the connections between sport and tourism are well established, this connection is gaining global significance. Media attention has more people becoming aware of the health and recreational benefits that sport and tourism provide … Spectator vacations are also increasingly popular with huge numbers of visitors attracted to sports events (DeKnop, 1998, p. 5).

Several attempts have been made in defining sport tourism, however it is unlikely that an authoritative definition will be presented until definitions have been accepted for sport and tourism as separate entities. Two examples of proposed definitions of sport tourism are those of Hall (1992), and Gibson, Attle, and Yiannakis (1998):

> Sport tourism falls into two categories, travel to participate in sport and travel to observe sport. Therefore, sport tourism may be defined as travel for non-commercial reasons, to participate or observe sporting activities away from the home range (Hall, 1992, p. 147).

> Travel away from one's primary residence to participate in a sport activity for recreation or competition, travel to observe sport at the grassroots level or elite level, and travel to visit a sport attraction such as a sports hall of fame or water park (Gibson et al., 1998, p. 53).

From these cited definitions, it can be summarised that sport tourism entails travel away from a person's home environment for the purpose of participating in, or observing sport. It should be noted that the definition proposed by Hall (1992) excludes professional athletes by inciting that sport tourism entails travel for non-commercial reasons, when other authors did include professional athletes in their suggested definitions, for example, Gibson (1998) and Hinch and Higham (2001).

Sport tourism was proposed by Zauhar (1996) to be a partnership between the world's largest social phenomenon, sport, and the world's largest industry, tourism, with this partnership providing mutual benefits for each other. Standeven and DeKnop (1999) agreed by describing sport tourism as a symbiotic relationship between the two phenomena. Standeven and DeKnop viewed sport and tourism as being interdependent, with sport being a special segment of the tourism industry, and also interactive as the relationship between the two can be influential on sports participation and infrastructure, and vice-versa in a tourism context.

Delpy (1998) proposed a model that suggested that sport tourism is composed of five primary niche markets: attractions, resorts, cruises, tours, and events. Delpy defined sport tourism events as 'those sports activities that attract a sizeable number of visiting participants and/or spectators…these sport tourism events have the potential to attract non-resident media and technical personnel such as coaches and officials' (p. 31). Other features that qualify a sport event to be touristic in nature were tourists travelling distances to see past and present sports stars or teams; tourists participating in or watching sport activities, formally planned or informally organised.

Sport tourism events of all levels are capable of attracting significant numbers of visitors, Burgan and Mules (1992) noted that 'in addition to their participants, sporting events often involve tourism numbers via spectators, participants' family and friends, media personnel, and officials' (p. 701). Associated with tourism influxes of sport tourism events, it is acknowledged that positive economic benefits can be accrued by a host community.

For example, the 2003 Rugby Union World Cup which was held in Australia, resulted in international visitors spending AU$410 million on tickets to the event and holiday expenditure. Australian residents purchased event tickets valued at AU$136.6 million and made nearly 180,000 interstate trips to attend World Cup matches, spending an estimated AU$142.6 million on interstate trip expenditure (URS Finance and Economics, 2004). An example of a smaller event (which fits into the category of major events) is the Gold Coast Airport Marathon. This event consistently attracts in excess of 8,000 runners plus their entourage to the Gold Coast each July and generates an estimated AU$6 million impact on the local economy (Getz & Fairley, 2004).

Additionally, sport tourism events are capable of promoting repeat visitation to a host community beyond the event itself, as Gibson (1998) explained:

> Another much touted benefit of hosting sports events is that they may promote tourism beyond the event itself. For example, people who attend the event may return for a vacation, or those who watch the event on television may decide to visit the destination later (p. 60)

It is also recognised that a sport tourism event held strategically during periods of low business, such as the off-season in regions that rely heavily on tourism to drive their economy, may be able to smooth out troughs in demand for tourist facilities such as restaurants and accommodation providers. Delpy (1998) noted that 'sport is seen as a new niche market with encouragement, particularly from hotels, as they see a major impact from events on their off-season and weekend business' (p. 33).

Section 2.7 has explored proposed definitions of sport tourism and sport tourism events. Additionally, the literature established sport tourism events as being one of five proposed niche markets of sport tourism. A discussion of the literature pertaining to sport tourism events was crucial to set boundaries around the type of events that are to be examined as part of this research. Section 2.8 presents the current knowledge regarding regional sport tourism events.

2.8 Regional Sport Tourism Events

Despite extensive acknowledgement and investigation of sport tourism events within the literature (Daniels, 2004; Daniels & Norman, 2003; Delpy, 1998; Higham, 1999), few authors have paid exclusive attention to sport tourism events held in regional areas, or on a local event scale, which for the purpose of the present study, shall be referred to as *regional sport tourism events*.

Much of the reviewed literature pertaining to regional events has presented several expressions to encapsulate events held at the local level. During their investigation of the economic impacts of the Northern Conference University Sports Association Games held in Lismore, New South Wales, Australia in 1995, Walo et al. (1996) labelled this event a 'local sports event' (p. 95). Meanwhile, Higham (1999) branded 'modest' (p. 87) sporting tournaments such as Masters Games, 'regular season sporting competitions' (p. 87). Long and Perdue (1990), who investigated the economic impact of a festival in a rural community, termed events at the community level, 'community festivals and special events' (p. 10). Murphy and Carmichael (1991) contrasted mega-events with smaller events which they referred to as 'small scale regional events' (p. 32). Delpy (1998), in her discussion of sport tourism events, referred to events held in less populated regions as 'smaller participative events' (p. 31). Finally, Daniels and Norman (2003) used 'local sport tourism events' (p. 215) as their preferred term for a regional sport tourism event. The wide variety of terms proposed by the above-cited authors suggests a level of perplexity exists amongst the academic fraternity as to the definition of a regional sport tourism event, hence the need for a universally accepted term.

In defining a regional sport tourism event, a definition of a *regional area* in Australia was proposed by Southern Cross University's Centre for Regional Tourism Research (2001) as 'those parts of Australia distant from the major international ports of entry' (p. iv). Additionally, Delpy (1998) proposed a definition of a sport tourism event, which states that sport tourism events are 'those sports activities that attract a sizeable number of visiting participants and/or spectators ... these sport tourism events have the potential to attract non-resident media and technical personnel such as coaches and officials' (p. 31). Thus, for the purpose of this research the definition of a regional sport tourism event is as follows:

> *Sports activities held on an infrequent basis, conducted in areas distant from major international ports of entry, that attract a sizeable number of visiting participants and/or spectators to the host community. Such events also have the potential to attract non-resident media, technical personnel and other sports officials.*

According to Walo et al. (1996), 'governments at all levels have increasingly turned to special events to promote tourism' (p. 96), this statement is echoed in the Australian Federal Government's *Draft National Sports Tourism Strategy*, which stated:

> Masters Games and 'manufactured' events can have significant impact at the regional and local level, as well as nationally. Indeed, there are numerous market sectors within sports tourism which lend themselves to regional areas and the lower level of facilities and infrastructure which these areas generally possess (Federal Department of Industry Science & Resources, 2000, p. 20).

Hosting a special event in a regional area can bring with it an array of positive benefits for the community: 'increases in employment, income, output, investment, extra services, infrastructure, and improvements. Intangible benefits such as growth in community spirit and cooperation can result from the host community being vitally involved in event planning and production' (Walo et al., 1996, p. 97). In a sport tourism event context, Daniels and Norman (2003) agreed by stating, 'regular sport tourism events offer great potential for host sites ... local residents with an interest in the given sport could enjoy one or several days of free entertainment' (p. 221).

Regional sport tourism events are popular with policy-makers in regional areas due to their ability to attract significant amounts of tourist expenditure to a local economy at a low cost to the host community (Daniels & Norman, 2003; Delpy, 1998; Dowell, 1999; Higham, 1999; Walo et al.,

1996). Additionally, Dowell (1999) felt that sport tourism events held in regional areas often make use of existing infrastructure. The Australian *National Draft Sports Tourism Strategy* named cycle races, triathlons and running races as examples of events that do not require specialised infrastructure to stage an event. The strategy document also suggested that once a town or region has created an event, that community then owns the event, which means it can be conducted on an annual basis thereby reducing the costs associated with running the event (Federal Department of Industry Science & Resources, 2000). This attribute of a regional sport tourism event is in contrast to a mega-event, which often requires construction of specialised infrastructure, expansion of tourist facilities, and the allocation of public funds away from other activities such as health or education, which bears an opportunity cost (Walo et al., 1996).

The popularity of hosting sport tourism events amongst regional communities is primarily attributed to the associated economic benefits of such events. A reflection of this popularity is found in that the majority of research into to this phenomenon has centred around the economic impact of events on host communities.

One such study was conducted by Daniels and Norman (2003), who investigated the economic benefits of seven sport tourism events in South Carolina, USA. Their study found that three of the seven events examined generated an injection to the host economy in excess of US$1 million, with the lowest recorded contribution being US$61,802. These figures serve to illustrate the contribution sport tourism events provide to regional economies. Additionally, Daniels and Norman (2003) found that over 90% of respondents visited the host region specifically for attending the sporting event.

Another study which investigated the economic impact of a regional sport tourism event was that of Walo et al. (1996). In determining the economic impact of the Northern Conference University Sports Association Games on its host region, Walo et al. found a net income for the Lismore area of AU$392,719 for the five-day event. These researchers also estimated a daily expenditure of AU$70.44 per visitor and a multiplier effect of 1:1.2, which meant 'for every dollar spent by visitors, another 20 cents was generated in income for the LCC [Lismore City Council] area' (p. 103).

Section 2.8 has established that no universal term or definition has been accepted for sport events held in regional areas that attract significant numbers of visitors to the host community. As such, a definition of a regional sport tourism event was proposed. The literature also established that it is possible for regional communities who host sport tourism events to accrue benefits such as an injection of new money into the local economy, increased employment, and smoothing out of demand for tourist facilities. Section 2.9 now presents a review of the literature examining event sponsorship.

2.9 Event Sponsorship

Contemporary society has evolved to see special events and sponsorship become synonymous to the point that as a society we 'have been programmed to judge any *un*sponsored event or activity as second-rate and of little significance' (Turner, 2001, p. 2). Concurrence exists amongst authorities in event management that sponsorship is vitally important to the financial viability of an event of any type (Allen et al., 2002; Carlsen, 2003; Crompton, 1993; Delpy et al., 1998).

Revenue to fund the staging of an event can stem from a range of sources. For example, Allen at al. (2002) have identified eight potential sources of revenue for special events. These included funds provided by the client; revenues sourced via fundraising efforts; grants; the sale of broadcast rights; on-site advertising revenues; profits from the sale of merchandise, ticket sales; and corporate sponsorship.

Of all forms of available event revenue sources, sponsorship is often an event's most significant source of income. It has been reported that on average 43% of any given event's budget was comprised of sponsorship funds (IEG, 1992a). This claim was reflected in a figure stated by the International Olympic Committee (2004), who reported that approximately 40% of revenue to fund each Olympic Games was sourced from corporate sponsorship.

The supposition proposed by McCarville and Copeland (1994) of sponsorship being an exchange relationship was echoed in an event sponsorship context by Crompton (1994). Crompton believed that each party (i.e. the event and the sponsor) both possess intrinsic needs that are able to be satisfied through a symbiotic relationship with one-another. For example, an event requires financial investment to fund its staging, whereas a business may yearn for increased brand awareness or for hospitality opportunities through which it can entertain valued clients. Through a sponsorship agreement, both parties are able to exchange resources on a reciprocal basis for mutual benefit.

Crompton (1995) stated that sponsorship of events grew 'exponentially' (p. 97) prior to the 1990's, and summarily offered nine influential factors which have driven the growth of event sponsorship. Many of these shared resemblance to Meenaghan's (1991) six driving forces behind the growth of commercial sponsorship presented in Section 2.3:

1. Rapid increases in the number of television channels, radio stations, magazines have meant that the impact of advertising messages have lost a lot of their impact on consumers due to advertising 'clutter'.

2. Escalating cost of television advertising, coupled with the advent of pay TV reducing the audience base of free-to-air television has meant that sponsorship is perceived to be more cost-efficient than television advertising. In concurrence with Meenaghan (1991), Crompton (1995) also felt that the ability of television audiences to tune out or fast-forward commercials has led to a decrease in the effectiveness of television advertising.

3. The introduction of colour television has increased the viewer appeal of televised events. Crompton (1995) wrote that sports events are popular with television stations as they are inexpensive to produce and are popular with television audiences.

4. The ban on tobacco and liquor advertising in the 1970s forced these industries to look elsewhere to promote their products. Again, a concurrent view with Meenaghan (1991). Crompton (1995) also stated that association of these harmful products with events gave the tobacco and liquor companies 'an aura of public respectability' (p. 98).

5. The commercialisation of sports events has become accepted by sports' organising bodies. Skinner and Rukavina (2003) agreed, in stating that it was only up until around the time of the 1984 Los Angeles Olympic Games that event managers realised that commercial sponsorship was the way forward in funding their events.

6. The successful sponsorships of the 1984 Los Angeles Olympic Games effectively legitimised sponsorship in the eyes of the corporate world as a promotional medium.

7. Acceptance of the concept of market segmentation meant that businesses realised that event sponsorship is an effective means of efficiently targeting specific market segments, as opposed to the more expensive and traditional method of mass marketing.

8. Increased competition and proliferation of products has led to consolidation of many companies via mergers and takeovers. This trend has meant that fewer but larger companies have control and influence in distribution channels. Thus it has become increasingly important for producers to maintain and enhance relations with distributors. Many companies have done so through sponsorship of events, which offer entertainment and communication benefits.

9. The final force that has stimulated the growth of event sponsorship according to Crompton (1995) was that increasingly, many cities are beginning to charge events for the use of city services such as police, fire and ambulance standbys, in addition to garbage collection. This increase in charges has caused a drain on event budgets and has meant that events are actively sourcing *more* sponsorship funds.

Crompton (1994) proposed that businesses generally sought four central benefits in sponsoring special events. They were 1) increased awareness, 2) image enhancement, 3) product trial or sales opportunities, and 4) hospitality opportunities (p. 70).

Increasing awareness of a business or brand can be achieved through sponsorship of an event. Crompton (1994) felt that this is particularly the case for new businesses or for new products, 'as sponsorship may be part of the overall promotion strategy to communicate its attributes to the target markets' (p. 70). Kuzma et al. (1993) agreed with Crompton's claim. Their survey of the Fortune 1,000 firms in the USA found that 'increase awareness of company' was the most frequently cited objective for sponsoring events amongst these businesses. Given that sponsors often use media coverage of an event as a vehicle to obtain exposure and increase awareness of a business or brand. Crowley (1991) felt that amending a sponsored event's title to reflect the association of the sponsor is a method of boosting a sponsor's exposure. However, if a business wished to achieve significant awareness at an event, the business should be cautious in becoming involved with an event that has a large portfolio of sponsors, as visibility as a sponsor may be impaired (Coughlan & Mules, 2001).

Crompton (1994) defined the term *image* as 'the mental construct developed by an individual on the basis of selected impressions' (p. 70). Despite suggesting that event sponsorship is unlikely to effectively change an image, Crompton maintained that companies still use event sponsorship to reinforce positive existing consumer images about their product or business. Crompton's view reflected Kuzma et al.'s (1993) findings, which rated 'improve company image' as the second most important event sponsorship objective by Fortune 1000 firms.

The opportunity to provide a sample or trial of a sponsor's product was another benefit frequently sought by businesses in event sponsorship according to Crompton (1994). The opportunity to sell products at an event through product trial can be very effective. Decker (1991) agreed with Crompton by stating that special events can provide a venue for sponsors 'to sell large quantities of product or service in a short period of time' (p. 45). Brooks (1994) noted that people 'attend events because they want to; therefore because they are relaxed and their guard is down, they are in a more receptive mood to receive product messages' (p. 167). Brooks also suggested that conditions at an event are conducive to selling product, as often a sponsor's product is exposed to consumers in an environment encompassing their lifestyles.

Hospitality opportunities were the final benefit sought by businesses that Crompton (1994) proposed. Often, events allocate sponsors free tickets to the event, combined with complementary food and beverages on the day as part of sponsors' benefits packages (2002). It is common for sponsoring businesses to invite esteemed or potential clients to their event and 'wine and dine' them in an attempt to 'create a personal interactive chemistry which will be conducive to doing business later' (Crompton, 1994, p. 71).

Section 2.9 established that sponsorship often represents a significant portion of many events' operating revenue, and that events are an extremely popular form of sponsorship investment in the corporate world. Event sponsorship's popularity was attributed by sponsorship researchers to factors such as the opportunity to offer product trials and consumers' receptivity to marketing messages when attending events. Section 2.10 moves on to present the literature examining the sponsorship of sport tourism events.

2.10 Sponsorship of Sport Tourism Events

To date, the literature pertaining to sponsorship of sport tourism events appears to be in the developing phase, as evidenced by Turco (1998), who stated, 'in light of the growth of sport sponsorships, and the increased popularity of sport tourism as a niche within the broader tourism industry, further analysis of the relationships of these subjects is required' (p. 14).

Of the many sponsorship opportunities available to the corporate world, sport tourism events have proven to be the most popular form of sponsorship investment (Delpy et al., 1998; Turco, 1998). IEG (1996) reported that of the US$5.9 billion spent on event sponsorship in North America, 65% of that figure was allocated to sport events. Owing to inefficiencies associated with purchasing advertising time during event telecasts, many businesses have elected to sponsor events themselves as opposed to paying for advertising in an attempt to achieve a higher return on investment (Turco, 1998). Meanwhile, Pope and Voges (1997) felt that sponsorship's proven abilities to overcome problems associated with traditional advertising methods and communicating with previously unreachable publics 'has seen the proliferation of corporate sponsorship of sporting events, and a large investment in advertising both at stadia and during telecasts of sporting events' (p. 16). Delpy et al. (1998) stated that most modern sport tourism events rely heavily upon corporate financial support to be successful.

In explaining why sport tourism events were the most popular form of sponsorship, Turco (1998) felt that product exclusivity was 'the sport tourism event marketer's prime asset, and it is not sold cheaply' (p. 14). This was a view shared by Skinner and Rukavina (2003) who stated that one of the most powerful weapons in an event managers' armoury is the ability to make a company the lone sponsor in its category. This can thereby allow that sponsor to differentiate itself from its competitors and lock out competitors from an event. However, product exclusivity as an event sponsorship benefit may open a door for a sponsor's competitors to undermine a rival business' sponsorship through a tactic known as *ambush marketing* (Crompton, 1993). Ambush marketing was defined by Sandler and Shani (1989) as 'a planned effort (campaign) by an organisation to associate themselves indirectly with an event in order to gain at least some of the recognition and benefits that are associated with being an official sponsor' (p. 10). Crompton (1993) stated that the primary objective of ambush marketing is *not* to gain exposure, while Sandler and Shani (1989) felt that the purpose is to create a misconception in the mind of the consumer as to who the sponsor really is and effectively weaken the impact of the legitimate sponsor's investment.

Sport tourism events offer a wide array of benefits and opportunities to sponsors. Delpy et al. (1998) suggested that the following are the primary benefits sought by businesses in sponsoring sport tourism events:

- Opportunities to introduce and promote new products to a marketplace;
- Differentiate and sell product;
- Reward sales staff;
- Entertain current and/or potential clients;
- Increase media and public exposure
- Enhance or change an image;
- Improve employee morale;
- Reach new market segments and distribution channels; and
- Lock out competitors.

Research by Carlsen (2003) into the reasons driving organisations to provide sponsorship to the Margaret River Masters Surfing Event in Western Australia, identified a wide assortment of objectives from the event's eight sponsors. Sponsors ranged in scope from local surf companies to government departments and multi-national organisations such as Coca Cola. Community involvement, brand/company awareness, brand positioning and media coverage were amongst the reasons cited by businesses for providing sponsorship to this event.

Section 2.10 found that sport tourism events are the most popular form of sponsorship investment by the corporate world, primarily owing to the increased television coverage that such events attract and the ability to lock out rival businesses from association from an event. The literature pertaining to sport tourism events provided little coverage of *why* businesses sponsor sport tourism events and *how* such sponsorships are managed, from both the sponsor and event manager's point of view. Thus, it is this gap in knowledge to which this research aims to contribute to. The following two sections examine operational functions of sponsorship, followed by an examination of the literature specifically related to the present study: SME sponsorship of regional sport tourism events.

2.11 Leveraging Event Sponsorships

Purchasing a sponsorship opportunity was widely considered to be ineffective in achieving communication objectives as a stand-alone technique. Numerous researchers advocated the practice of investing additional funds in activities designed to capitalise on a sponsorship investment (Abratt & Grobler, 1989; Arthur, Scott, Woods, & Booker, 1998; Meenaghan, 1991; Pope & Voges, 1994). Abratt et al. (1987) stated that sponsorship should not be used on its own. It should instead be utilised in conjunction with a firm's advertising campaign 'in order to achieve the maximum benefit from both activities' (p. 306). Sleight (1989) agreed, in stating:

> It is a rare sponsorship indeed that can provide anything more than a temporary effect on these factors [changes to image, brand awareness] unless run over a long period and supported by all the communications tools at the marketer's disposal to supply the continuous reinforcement that these factors require (p. 82).

This practice is known as *leveraging*, which Meenaghan (1991) defined as 'the additional effort, largely promotional, which must be invested by the sponsor in order to properly exploit the opportunity provided as a result of securing particular sponsorship rights' (p. 43). Research by Pope and Voges (1997) into sponsor recall rates at rugby league's 1994 State of Origin clearly confirmed that 'promoting the promotion' (p. 25) on the sponsors' part results in higher recall and recognition of brand names associated with a sport. Crompton (1993) felt that sponsorship is effective in this manner as it provides a 'hook – a focus or unifying theme – to which the other communication vehicles can relate' (p. 100). For example, photographs or video footage of the sponsorship may be taken and then integrated into subsequent advertising campaigns.

With regard to the amount of additional funds that should be spent by sponsors in leveraging their sponsorships, Meenaghan (2001) claimed that it is 'generally accepted' (p. 192) that a sum at least equal to the initial cost of obtaining the sponsorship rights should be allocated to leveraging activities. Sleight (1989) also shared this view in suggesting that if a sponsor does not allocate a promotional spend at least equal to the sponsorship fee, then the sponsor was not spending enough to secure the proper level of benefits for itself, as opposed to the event. Meerabeau et al. (1991) concurred in stating that 'back-up exploitation ... should match the contract cost pound for pound...in order to get maximum benefit' (p. 50). Given the statements of these authors, it is fair to suggest that the cost of a sponsorship package is merely a cost of entry. In fact, Sandler and Shani (1993) felt that Olympic Games sponsors 'in effect, just 'bought a licence' to spend more money to exploit this fact' (p. 39).

Having established the necessity to leverage a sponsorship if the full potential of the arrangement is to be exploited, how does one go about leveraging a sponsorship? Parker (1991) noted that the execution of leveraging techniques varies widely according to the type of sponsorship. However, common techniques employed were:

- Production of merchandise;
- Advertising;
- Promotions;
- Competitions;
- On-pack signage; and
- Point-of-sale material.

An extremely popular sport attracting sponsorship in the USA is NASCAR automobile racing. Corbett and Lekush (2003) stated that sponsors leverage their sponsorship of racing teams through media relations, public relations campaigns, at-track VIPs and hospitality, business-to-business promotions and new product development. Corbett and Lekush felt that properly leveraged sponsorships aid in reinforcing a company's link to a driver and increases product loyalty amongst consumers (p. 20).

Another example of leveraging a sponsorship is that of the American brewing company, Coors, and its sponsorship of a racing team on the NASCAR Winston Cup circuit. The leveraging activities undertaken by this firm are highlighted in bold. Coors wished to promote its new beer, Keystone through this sponsorship. The first phase of the promotion revolved around the introduction of 12 packs of beer, which **advertised the sponsorship** on the physical packaging. The actual beer cans **carried the Winston Cup schedule** on them **(on-pack signage)**, and the 12 packs were delivered to retailers a few weeks prior to the Daytona 500 race. Special 12 pack displays of Keystone beer were distributed to retail outlets in the target regions **(point-of-sale material)**, and a **sweepstakes competition** was promoted through **point-of-sale** materials at retailers (IEG, 1992b).

Neglecting to leverage a sponsorship has been linked with sponsorship failure in the past. Amis, Slack and Berrett (1999) found that a clothing company provided sponsorship to a range of high-profile sporting events by way of providing a large amount of expensive sport clothing free of charge. However, the sponsor made no attempt to leverage their association and thus netted a nil return on investment. The marketing manager of the firm in question remarked in hindsight, 'just putting a tag on a coat ain't gonna cut it, and that's all that was done' (p. 264).

Crompton (1993) noted that event organisers frequently disregard the fact that other communications tools must be utilised in order for a sponsor to obtain maximum benefit from its sponsorship. This was attributed to leveraging often being considered by event organisers as an indirect cost of sponsorship, which sponsors should bear, thereby significantly increasing the cost of a sponsorship. Crompton suggested that when planning an event, organisers would do best to consider how they can assist a sponsor's overall communications strategy, as opposed to taking a narrow-minded approach of how they can help the sponsor maximise its in-site investment. This view was shared by Brooks (1994) who felt that the organisers of minor sports events have been slow to recognise the value of corporate promotional spending, and such organisers should allow sponsors the use of the exploitable properties of their event to aid in event promotion.

Section 2.11 established that sponsorship as a stand-alone technique is inadequate, and that leveraging techniques designed to complement a sponsor's overall communications strategy are necessary in order for a sponsor to exploit the maximum benefit from their sponsorship investment. Common leveraging techniques included merchandising, advertising of the sponsorship, associated promotions and competitions and point-of-sale material. Little has been written regarding the leveraging practices of SMEs sponsoring regional sport tourism events, and as such it this gap in the literature that inspired the third research objective of the present study. Section 2.12 now examines the literature relevant to the evaluation of sponsorship effectiveness.

2.12 Evaluation of Sponsorship Effectiveness

The literature pertaining to sponsorship has affirmed that sponsorship is acutely dissimilar to the notions of philanthropy or altruism, in that a commercial return *is* expected by the sponsor as the principal outcome of such an arrangement (Bennett, 1997; Copeland et al., 1996; Crompton, 1997). In satisfying a sponsor that a commercial return has been obtained, many experts advocated the evaluation of sponsorships in the aftermath of a sponsorship arrangement. Arthur et al. (1998) felt that the shift of corporate attitudes towards sponsorship being a bottom-line oriented practice and away from altruism, was a driving factor in the increased importance placed on the evaluation of sponsorships by the corporate world. Stotlar (2004) stated that the evaluation of a sponsorship essentially centred around satisfying the sponsor that an appropriate level of value has been reciprocated between the two parties engaged in a sponsorship.

The issue of sponsorship evaluation within the literature was contentious, and it was clear that little agreement existed amongst researchers in this discipline as to how evaluation should take place, by whom, and what methods of evaluation were available. Crompton (2004) stated that the literature pertaining to sponsorship evaluation was 'underdeveloped … it consists of anecdotal information and case studies from which it is difficult to make useful generalisations' (p. 268). Meanwhile, Arthur et al. described the topic of sponsorship evaluation as an issue that has 'vexed authors for a number of years' (pp. 55-56). Carter and Wilkinson (2000) attributed a perceived lack of evaluation by sponsoring companies to 'the lack of appropriate measures of effectiveness of sponsorship' (p. 176).

Kuzma et al. (1993) summarised the importance of sponsorship evaluation in stating, 'the importance of follow-up by the event organisers cannot be emphasised too strongly. Every attempt must be made to provide the sponsor with the satisfaction promised' (p. 32), while Geldard and Sinclair (1996) proposed that 'the need to provide investment accountability to your sponsors is more and more becoming a critical part of the sales deal' (p. 263).

Arthur et al. (1998) felt that any sponsorship program should be undertaken with a set of SMART (Specific, Measurable, Attainable, Relevant, and Trackable) objectives in place to guide the sponsorship, thus any evaluation technique employed should relate back to these objectives. Meenaghan (1991) shared this view by stating, 'final evaluation must take place when the sponsorship is completed to determine performance levels against the stated objectives' (p. 44). From the views of these authors, the inference is clear: with no objectives in place, determining the success of a sponsorship is very difficult.

Despite the increasing importance placed on sponsorship's bottom-line orientation, the evaluation of sponsorship programs has been viewed as somewhat insignificant to many corporations (Stotlar, 2004). Kuzma and Shanklin (1994) stated that many companies did not evaluate their sponsorships owing primarily to the fact that they have not yet found a useful method for doing so. However,

Abratt and Grobler (1989) found otherwise during their empirical work investigating the sponsorship evaluation practices of twenty-eight South African businesses. These authors discovered that in fact many businesses *did* evaluate their sponsorships, albeit in a very informal and non-systematic fashion.

Techniques used to evaluate sponsorships have certainly progressed since the early days of sponsorship. The 'gut feeling' method of evaluation was common in the 1980s, however, Geldard and Sinclair (1996) stated that this method was flawed because no tangible proof of effectiveness could be provided to the sponsor. The 'gut feeling' method can be directly contrasted to the model proposed by Stotlar (2004). Stotlar's model suggested a systematic process of evaluation whereby the initial objectives of the sponsorship were identified, along with the methods of achieving the stated objectives through the property. The outcomes of the sponsorship are scrutinised through a mix of quantitative techniques to determine if the sponsor's objectives were achieved or not.

Meenaghan (1991) proposed five methods for conducting an evaluation of sponsorship effectiveness. They were 1) measuring the level of media coverage/exposure gained, 2) measuring the communications effectiveness of sponsorship involvement, 3) measuring the sales effectiveness of sponsorship, 4) monitoring guest feedback, and 5) cost-benefit analysis. These methods are summarised below.

1) Measuring the level of media coverage/exposure gained

The level of media coverage or exposure gained was seen by some sponsors as an indication of sponsorship effectiveness. Often, the duration of television and radio coverage, in addition to print media coverage (expressed in column inches) were determinants of success when utilising media coverage as an appraisal tool (Meenaghan, 1991). Work by Pope and Voges (1994) substantiated the popularity of media exposure amongst sponsors as a performance indicator. These authors found that eight out of the eleven sponsors using evaluation that they surveyed, named 'media audit' as their preferred form of evaluation. However, Speed and Thompson (2000) concluded that this method of evaluation was problematic as it is post hoc and ineffective in aiding management decisions regarding future sponsorships.

2) Measuring the communications effectiveness of sponsorship involvement

Communications effectiveness pertains to impacts upon the consumer of awareness and perceived image of the sponsoring company/brand. In utilising this factor as an evaluative tool, 'levels of awareness achieved, attitudes created, perceptions changed or associations suggested are measured against stated objectives' (Meenaghan, 1991, p. 44).

3) Measuring the sales effectiveness of sponsorship

Such a technique involves measuring the impact upon sales resulting from a sponsorship. However, Meenaghan (1991) believed that to actually carry out such an evaluation is difficult and is often imprecise. Sleight (1989) agreed, and believed that this method of evaluation was only possible if *all* variables in the business' communications mix are held constant such as product price, quality and availability, as a change in any of these factors may result in a skewed evaluation outcome. Brooks (1994) identified factors such as fluctuating economic conditions and actions of competitors as also contributing to the lack of reliability of sales impacts as a performance indicator.

4) Monitoring guest feedback

Given that many companies engage in sponsorship with the provision of client hospitality as a key objective (Crompton, 1994), Meenaghan (1991) felt that the monitoring of guest opinions can be an important indicator of sponsorship success. Meenaghan also believed that spectators, participants and event organisers are valuable feedback sources for sponsorship evaluation.

5) Cost-benefit analysis

The final method of sponsorship evaluation proposed by Meenaghan (1991) was the cost-benefit analysis. Geldard and Sinclair (1996) depicted a cost-benefit analysis as a process whereby the costs of the sponsorship are totalled, and the value of the benefits received are subtracted. The ensuing figure should then be compared against an industry benchmark. This comparison yields an indication of how effectively the sponsorship has been managed.

In an alternative approach based upon content analysis of sponsorship industry publications, Crompton (2004) found that larger businesses that spend significant amount of money on sport sponsorship evaluated the effectiveness of their sponsorships through five broad approaches. They were:

1. Measuring media equivalencies;
2. Measuring impact on awareness;
3. Measuring impact on image;
4. Measuring impact on intent to purchase; and
5. Measuring impact on sales (source: Crompton, 2004, pp. 272-278).

There appeared to be no right or wrong way to evaluate a sponsorship. The extent to which a sponsor will evaluate will vary according to the scope of the investment, as Arthur et al. (1998) stated, 'the actual methods of evaluation will depend to a great extent on the level of sponsorship, with those of a higher financial contribution attracting a far more rigorous and complex evaluation than those involving less expenditure' (p. 57). Additionally, the data available and the information required by the sponsor will be influential in selecting an evaluation method (Kuzma & Shanklin, 1994). It is also unclear *who* is responsible for conducting the evaluation. Geldard and Sinclair (1996) spoke of evaluation reports that should be prepared by the sponsored party and presented to the sponsor, which suggested that these authors felt that the sponsored party was responsible for conducting the evaluation.

Upon the completion of the investigative phase of a sponsorship evaluation, Geldard and Sinclair (1996) considered it necessary for an event to prepare a précis report of the sponsorship for its sponsor. They proposed four levels of reporting, each progressing in complexity according to the amount of support a sponsor has provided. Copeland et al. (1996) lend support to the argument that event managers should prepare and distribute a report on sponsorship effectiveness to its sponsors were. These authors felt that instead of expecting a sponsor to undertake an evaluation, sport event organisers who take the initiative in conducting some or all of the evaluation will 'place themselves in a more competitive position' (p. 46) for renewing sponsorship contracts and attracting further sponsorship. Stotlar (2004) stated that when events did attempt to provide a sponsorship effectiveness report to sponsors, such reports 'often pay little attention to the sponsor's objectives, but rather detail only attendance figures and media impressions' (p. 62).

Section 2.12 established that the evaluation of sponsorships has emerged from the shift of sponsorship as an altruistic practice to a bottom-line orientation. As yet, no one authoritative process of evaluation has been proposed. Of the few that do appear in the literature, most suggest that the objectives set by the sponsor should form the basis for determining if a sponsorship has been successful or not. Media exposure levels, communications effectiveness, sales impact, guest opinions and cost-benefit analysis were techniques that have been proposed as tools for sponsorship appraisal. However, conjecture exists as to which of these was the most robust indicator of sponsorship effectiveness. The fourth objective of this research is 'to explore if and how event managers and sponsors evaluated the effectiveness of their sponsorship agreement', thus necessitating a review of literature examining sponsorship evaluation. It was from a gap in the evaluation literature that the fourth research objective originated, as little attention had been paid to the evaluation practices within sponsorship agreements between SMEs and regional sport tourism events. Section 2.13 now presents the literature regarding SME sponsorship of regional sport tourism events.

2.13 SME Sponsorship of Regional Sport Tourism Events

Crowley (1991) has noted that sponsorship of regional sports events is a popular communications medium in the corporate world 'because the sponsorship of local events is much prized as an integrative medium whereby the business marries its persona with that of the local community' (p. 14). When compared to a 'big business' and 'big event' context, there is little known about small and medium business' involvement in providing sponsorship to regional sport tourism events. Slack and Bentz (1996) felt that 'small businesses are extensively involved in the sponsorship of sports teams and events. However, there has been virtually no examination of the rationale for this involvement' (p. 175).

One of the few empirical studies into this issue was undertaken by Mount and Niro (1995). These investigators examined SME sponsorship of three sports events in regional Canada, in which twenty-nine small businesses were surveyed over the weekend that these three events were held. Areas of inquiry pertained to reasons for sponsoring the events; audience being targeted through this sponsorship; leveraging activities associated with the sponsorships; and evaluation of the effectiveness of the sponsorships.

In identifying the reasons driving small and medium businesses to provide sponsorship to these events, Mount and Niro (1995) found that 'helps build/reinforce name recognition' and 'demonstrates good corporate citizenship' as the two most frequent responses. The least important reason cited was 'to compete outside of marketplace' with other businesses. These findings are summarised in Table 2.2.

Leveraging activities employed by the sponsoring businesses were also investigated by Mount and Niro, however such activities were referred to as 'tie-in support activities'. It was found that 70% of respondents spent money on leveraging their sponsorship investment, with advertising their sponsorship of the event and in-store displays being the most frequently employed methods of leveraging. Other leveraging methods included the distribution of free tickets to events, in-store promotions, and donating prizes to be given away at the event.

In evaluating the effectiveness of their sponsorship investment, Mount and Niro (1995) found that 81% of respondents indicated that they did conduct some sort of evaluation. The most commonly employed methods of evaluation included feedback from customers, observation of increased or decreased in-store traffic, and the success of the event.

Table 2.2: **Reported reasons for sponsorship by SMEs (source: Mount & Niro, 1995, p. 172).**

Reason for sponsorship	%
Helps build/reinforce name recognition	30
Demonstrates good corporate citizenship	26
Good advertising vehicle	22
Event complemented nature of the business	15
Generates excellent publicity	11
Image of the event (e.g. positive family image)	7
Produces favourable media interest	4
To compete outside of marketplace	0
Other	7

Mount and Niro (1995) concluded that their results paralleled previous findings of big business sponsorship studies in that increasing brand awareness is an important factor in providing sponsorship to an event, and that leveraging of sponsorships was common practice amongst small, medium and large businesses. However, these authors noted that businesses in a small town setting realised the important role special events play in their community in terms of improving quality of life for local residents by way of stimulating local economies and enhancing community cohesion. Such small businesses often acknowledge that special events in their community would most likely not exist without their support through sponsorship.

Work by Slack and Bentz (1996) was the other significant piece of research into the sponsorship of sports events by small businesses. These authors conducted qualitative, semi-structured interviews with the managers of eleven small businesses whom were located in a large western Canadian city. Interview questions pertained to how sponsorship requests were processed; who makes the decision to sponsor a cause or not; the rationale for providing sponsorship; and how such sponsorships were evaluated.

Slack and Bentz (1996) found that the decision to sponsor a cause or not was generally a one-person decision made by the owner/manager of the business and that 'there were no formalised procedures to guide the sponsorship decisions' (p. 178). Personal contacts and interests of the business' manager were also found to be influential in a decision to sponsor a team or event. Business managers were more likely to sponsor sports teams or events with whom the manager has personal contacts, or in which the manager has a personal interest in the given sport or activity.

Many of Slack and Bentz's (1996) respondents indicated a desire for a return on their sponsorship investments, nullifying any proposition that small businesses provide sponsorship to sports events for altruistic reasons. One respondent remarked that if 'you want people to come back through the door ... just give them something and they're gone, what good is that? We need to get them back in' (p. 179). Having expressed that they desire a return on investment, it was also found that many respondents made use of leveraging and evaluation techniques associated with their sponsorships. One sponsor was a jewellery store who provided substantial sponsorship to women's' sports events:

> As well as providing cash or prizes for events they would also provide vouchers for free ring cleaning, chain soldering, or jewellery appraisal. This had the effect of driving in-store traffic and by counting the number of vouchers used it was also possible to provide a very crude evaluation of the success of the sponsorship (Slack & Bentz, 1996, p. 179).

Corporate social responsibility and business image was the most frequently cited reason for engaging in sport event sponsorship amongst Slack and Bentz' respondents. Respondents were typically under the impression that engaging in sponsorship of community sports events brings about credibility and positive exposure within the local community for the sponsoring business, as the business is seen to be 'making a contribution to the community's social and economic well being' (p. 181). Abratt et al. (1987) partially agreed with these findings and wrote, 'local event sponsorships have limited appeal and the majority of these are undertaken by the sponsors mainly as a result of their awareness of social responsibility to their respective communities: mass exposure is not sought' (p. 304).

Community sport event sponsorship was also seen to be an influential factor for non-consumer audiences such as politicians, local media and financial institutions. One small business owner pointed out:

> If you're involved in these things and the mayor or alderman are at them, you get to develop some sort of personal rapport and then you can pick up the phone and say 'look we've got this problem'. Because of the things we've done they return the call that much quicker (Slack & Bentz, 1996, p. 181).

In contrast to Mount and Niro (1995), who found that using sponsorship of local sports events to compete with rival businesses in a marketplace was uncommon, Slack and Bentz' (1996) data suggested that it was common for small businesses to sponsor events in order to differentiate themselves from competitors and gain a competitive advantage. It was also revealed that sponsorship of community sports events were often used as a reactive strategy, 'when they see rival companies getting involved in sponsorships the owner/managers of small businesses often follow suit in order to neutralise any competitive advantage that may be gained by the company making the first sponsorship' (p. 182).

Section 2.13 found that SMEs sponsored regional sport tourism events in order to obtain credibility and be seen making a contribution to their local communities. Such sponsors did not engage in sponsorship for altruistic purposes. This was evidenced by the frequent use of leveraging activities and evaluation of sponsorship investments on the part of the sponsoring business. It was from gaps in this literature that two of the research objectives for the present study emerged. Firstly, there was no coverage of sponsor or event managers' perceptions of sponsorship, or how such agreements were initiated.

2.14 Chapter Summary

This chapter has provided a review of the available literature pertaining to the sponsorship of regional sport tourism events by SMEs. The generic issue of sponsorship, its definition, and its place in the marketing communications mix were examined, along with issues relating to special events, sport tourism event and specifically, regional sport tourism events and the sponsorship of such phenomena. Two operational functions of sponsorship: leveraging and evaluation were also discussed with reference to an event context. Chapter Three now provides details of the methodology constructed to achieve the research objectives stated in Chapter One.

CHAPTER THREE

METHODOLOGY

3.1 Introduction

The purpose of this chapter is to document the research methods employed to achieve the underlying objectives of this research which were introduced in Chapter One. It was deemed appropriate that an interpretive, qualitative, multiple case study approach be adopted for achieving the objectives of this research. Justification for the choice of this methodology is provided in detail throughout this chapter.

The methodology of this research involved identifying a sample of all events within the research area that met the definition of a regional sport tourism event, from which six events were initially selected for participation. Qualitative, semi-structured interviews were conducted with the event managers of selected cases. Upon completion of each interview the event manager was asked to identify businesses that provided sponsorship to their event. One sponsor from each event was then pursued and asked to participate in the study. Upon agreeing to participate, a qualitative semi-structured interview was conducted with the manager of the respective business. Collected interview data was then transcribed and analysed utilising a three-stage process of analysis proposed by Miles and Huberman (1994). Justification for the use of this research strategy is provided in this chapter.

3.2 Research Paradigm

According to Jennings (2001), a paradigm can be described as 'the overlying view of the way of the world works' (p. 34). Jennings also stated that six paradigms exist which guide social science research. These include positivism; the interpretive social science approach; critical theory orientation; feminist perspectives; the postmodern approach; and chaos theory orientation (Jennings, 2001, p. 33).

In defining which paradigm a specific research study is grounded in, Guba (1990) suggested that three questions be asked of the research and the researcher, based upon the ontological, epistemological and methodological bases of the research. The ontological question asks how the researcher views the nature of the 'knowable' or, what is the researcher's perception of the nature of 'reality'? The epistemological inquiry addresses the nature of the relationship between the knower (the inquirer) and the known (or knowable). Lastly, the methodology query refers to the way in which the inquirer should go about finding out knowledge (Guba, 1990).

Table 3.1 applies Guba's (1990) three questions to the two main research paradigms: positivism and interpretive social sciences, which assists in justifying why this study is grounded within the interpretive social sciences paradigm. Guba's three considerations are now discussed in light of this study into sponsorship agreements between regional sport tourism events and SMEs.

Table 3.1: An overview of two informative paradigms (source: adapted from Jennings, 2001, p. 56).

	Positivism	Interpretive Social Sciences
Ontology	Universal truths and laws	Multiple realities
Epistemology	Objective	Subjective
Methodology	Quantitative	Qualitative

Ontologically, multiple explanations for the phenomena under investigation may exist due to a lack of previous research into SME sponsorship of regional sport tourism events, which according to Table 3.1 suggests that a positivist approach may be inappropriate for this study. In an epistemological sense, this research involved the researcher entering the social setting of event managers and SME business managers in order to gain an empathetic understanding of the sponsorship relationship between the two parties. The findings are a creation of the process of the interaction between the researcher and the researched (Guba, 1990), and are therefore subjective. Owing to the subjective interaction between the researcher and the participants, further justification is added to this study being grounded within an interpretive paradigm, as a positivist approach entails an objective interaction (Jennings, 2001). Methodologically, a qualitative approach will satisfy the exploratory research objectives of this study whereas a quantitative approach may not, owing to the small number of events available to be studied. Further, much previous research into event sponsorship has been quantitative, and a qualitative approach may address this issue by yielding more comprehensive data. It is from the points raised in this paragraph that justify why this study into sponsorship agreements between SMEs and regional sport tourism events is grounded within the interpretive social sciences paradigm.

Section 3.2 established this research investigating SME sponsorship of regional sport tourism events as being grounded within the interpretive social sciences paradigm. Justification was provided on the basis of statements from Guba (1990) and Jennings (2001). Section 3.3 now presents a justification for the use of a case study research approach for this study.

3.3 Case Studies and Conditions for use of Case Studies

When selecting a research strategy, Yin (2003) proposed three factors that should be considered. The first factor was the form of the research question (i.e. whether it is a 'who', 'what', 'where', 'when', 'why' or 'how' question). The second factor asked whether the researcher required control over behavioural events of the participants, and finally, whether the research focused on contemporary events was the third factor to be considered when selecting a research strategy. Yin (2003, p. 5) applied these three considerations to five research strategies: experiments, surveys, archival analyses, histories and case studies which aids in justifying why a case study strategy was selected for this research into SME sponsorship of regional sport tourism events.

Yin's (2003) three considerations were integral in the decision to employ case studies as the research approach for this study. First, the objectives of this research were asking 'how' and 'why' questions of its participants, such as 'how' sponsors and event managers perceive sponsorship, and 'why' SMEs sponsor regional sport tourism events. As such, a survey and archival analysis were eliminated as possible research strategies. Second, the researcher did not require control over the behaviour of event managers and business managers as the research was examining past behaviour of such persons. Thus, an experiment was eliminated, which left a case study or historical approach as possible research strategies. Finally, the research was examining contemporary events, which meant that based upon the Yin's three considerations, the most suitable research strategy for this study was a case study approach.

Case study approaches involve the researcher carefully selecting one or a few key cases to illustrate an issue and analytically study it (Neuman, 2003). Adding strength to the decision to adopt a case study approach, Neuman (2003) felt that case study data were usually more detailed, varied and extensive while Yin (2003) suggested that case studies were 'the preferred strategy when "how" or "why" questions are being posed' (p. 1), as was the case with this research.

Section 3.3 outlined the decision-making process in selecting a case study research approach for the present study which investigates SME sponsorship of regional sport tourism events. Justification for their use was provided by statements from Neuman (2003) and Yin (2003). Section 3.4 now documents the case study procedures constructed to guide this research.

3.4 Case Study Procedures

Section 3.4 describes the case study procedures undertaken in this study, while Section 3.4.1 outlines how appropriate events and sponsors were selected and approached for participation in this research.

3.4.1 Selection of cases

The selection of cases for this study was undertaken in a two-stage process. The first stage in this process involved selecting appropriate events suitable for inclusion in the research, while the second stage involved selecting appropriate businesses (sponsors) for inclusion. The process of selecting these two groups is detailed in Sections 3.4.1.1 and 3.4.1.2.

3.4.1.1 Selection of event cases

In order to select appropriate events to investigate, a list of sport tourism events held within the geographical research area was compiled. From this list, a sample of events was selected using a purposive selection process. Approximately thirty sport tourism events suitable for inclusion in this study existed within the geographical research area. In order for the researcher to accurately identify the sampling frame, it was necessary to compile a list of sport tourism events in the research area. The need to compile this list was due to the absence of an already published list that was comprehensive enough to illustrate the range of sport tourism events in the research area. In compiling the list of sport tourism events in the research area, a number of information sources were utilised, namely local government web sites, local media web sites, sporting organisation web sites; regional event calendars, tourism agency web sites, and published sport directories.

As a result, Table 3.2 was conceived, which illustrates the sampling frame of this study. Purposive sampling was chosen as an appropriate sampling method for this research. Jennings (2001) stated that purposive sampling is a non-probability form of sampling that:

> Involves the researcher making a decision about who or what study units will be involved in the study. The researcher uses their knowledge to determine who or what study units are the most appropriate for inclusion in the study based on the potential study units' knowledge base or closeness of fit to criteria associated with the study's focus (p.139).

Neuman (2003) added strength to the decision to use a purposive method of selecting cases by stating that purposive sampling is suitable 'when a researcher wants to identify particular types of cases for in-depth investigation' (p. 213). Further, Creswell (1994) suggested that 'the idea of qualitative research is to purposefully select informants that will best answer the research questions. No attempt is made to randomly select informants' (p. 148).

Cases were purposively selected from Table 3.2. Miles and Huberman (1994) stated that it is necessary to set boundaries when undertaking qualitative research, and to define aspects of the cases that can be investigated within the researcher's time and means. Consequently, the researcher imposed a set of criteria upon events being targeted for participation. Criteria for purposively selecting participants for the study were based upon two factors: 1) the type of sport in focus, and 2) the geographical location of the event.

The type of sport in focus was the second factor in purposively selecting events for participation in the study. The researcher felt that richer, more meaningful data may be collected through targeting a mix of different sport tourism events for interviewing. This was so as to not include for example, mostly cricket events or mostly surfing events as the sample.

The second factor in purposively selecting events was geographical location. Similar in reasoning to the 'type of sport in focus', an even spread of events held in coastal towns (in which, many events were water-based) and inland areas was sought after. Again, this was to ensure an adequate mix of sport tourism event typologies were included in the study.

Upon selecting purposively selecting six events and identifying the event manager from each, a mailing package was forwarded to each event manager that contained a cover letter requesting their participation in the study. In addition, an informed consent form was supplied, outlining the specific details of the study and the requirements of participants. This form made the participant aware that their responses may be quoted in written accounts of the research; assured the participant anonymity; and reassured them that any quoted responses could not be traced back to them. The Southern Cross University Human Research Ethics Committee approved all content of the mailing packages, as well as all aspects of the research proposal.

Table 3.2: Sport tourism events within the research area.

EVENT	LOCATION	SPORT
Seagulls Duathlon	Tweed Heads	Duathlon
Speed on Tweed Festival	Murwillumbah	Motor Racing
Masters Easter Road Carnival	Murwillumbah	Cycling
Tweed River Bridge to Bridge Swim Classic	Murwillumbah	Swimming
Australian Country Cricket Championships	Lismore	Cricket
Far North Coast Junior Cricket Carnival	Lismore	Cricket
USA v Australia Test	Lismore	Motor Racing
Australian National Baseball Championships	Lismore	Baseball
Parramatta v Cronulla NRL Trial Game	Lismore	Rugby League
Easter Tennis Classic	Lismore	Tennis
Lismore Junior Round Robin Tennis Classic	Lismore	Tennis
City v Country Origin Game	Lismore	Rugby League
Rainbow Region Masters Games	Lismore	Masters Sport
Lismore Cup	Lismore	Horse Racing
Byron Bay Easter Surf Classic	Byron Bay	Surfing
Winter Whales Byron Bay Ocean Swim	Byron Bay	Swimming
Byron Bay Triathlon	Byron Bay	Triathlon
Byron Bay Malibu Classic	Byron Bay	Surfing
All Girls Surf Showdown	Lennox Head	Surfing
Rusty Gromfest	Lennox Head	Surfing
'Fair Go' Skate Competition & Music Festival	Ballina	Skating
Wardell Half Marathon	Wardell	Running
Evans Head Triathlon	Evans Head	Triathlon
Evans Head Seafood Bowls Carnival	Evans Head	Lawn Bowls
Pippi Beach Surf Classic	Yamba	Surfing
Red Rock/Corindi Triathlon	Red Rock	Triathlon
Woolgoolga Triathlon	Woolgoolga	Triathlon
Bananacoast Triathlon	Coffs Harbour	Triathlon
Coffs Harbour Ocean Swims	Coffs Harbour	Swimming

3.4.1.2 Selection of business (sponsor) cases

Upon completion of an interview with an event manager, the manager was asked to identify the names of businesses that provided his or her event with cash or in-kind sponsorship for the *most recent* running of their event prior to the interview taking place. Interviewees were also asked at this point which of the identified sponsors they felt would be the most receptive to an invitation to participate in the research, and which sponsor may provide the most useful information with regard to this study. In all cases, the interviewee was happy to provide this information, and the sponsor perceived by the event manager to be the most receptive and informative was forwarded a mail package requesting their participation in the research.

As with selecting events, criteria for selecting SME sponsors for participation in the research were imposed by the researcher. Initially, businesses identified by event managers upon completion of an interview were categorised as *small* or *medium* businesses according to the Australian Bureau of Statistics (2001) definition of such enterprises which stated that:

> Small businesses are defined as businesses employing less than 20 people in all industries except agriculture where the definition is businesses with an EVAO [estimated value of agricultural operations] of between $22,500 and $400,000 (p. 124).

> Medium businesses (excluding agriculture) are defined as businesses employing 20 or more people but less than 200 (p. 123).

In addition to meeting the definition of small or medium business as proposed by the Australian Bureau of Statistics (2001), businesses targeted for participation must have satisfied the following criteria in order to be included.

- Must have been in a current arrangement with a regional sport tourism event in which the business provides cash or in-kind support; and
- Must have sponsored its respective event for at least one running of the event.

In the event where a business belonged to a franchise or chain of businesses, it was resolved that if the funds allocated to sponsor an event originated from the coffers of the local branch or agency (such as a local real estate agent or bank branch) then that business would be eligible to participate in the research. Where funds originated from the coffers of the franchise or chain's central management, that business would be included in the research only if the chain as a whole employed less than 200 persons. This process was adopted to preserve the SME context of this research.

Upon determining that identified businesses satisfied the imposed criteria, the selected businesses were forwarded a mailing package (individually addressed to the person identified by the respective event manager) requesting their participation in the study, along with an informed consent form. A follow-up telephone call was made one week after the mailing package was posted to each respective business to confirm receipt of the mail package and as an attempt to build some prior rapport with the potential participant.

It was suggested by Yin (2003) that when conducting qualitative research, enquiry should be conducted to the point of *literal replication*, which is the point where no new information is being generated. Initially, six events were purposively selected from Table 3.2 and were asked to participate in the research. After ten interviews (five case studies) had been conducted and data transcribed, condensed and analysed, no significant new information was being generated. At this point, the researcher elected to cease data collection and the total number of case studies that were to form the basis of this research stood at five.

Section 3.4 has documented and justified the case study procedures employed to conduct this research. Section 3.5 now discusses the strategy chosen to collect the required data from the research participants.

3.5 Data Collection

This section describes and justifies the data collection process that was adopted for this research into SME sponsorship of regional sport tourism events. Interview typologies are discussed in Section 3.5.1, followed by justification for the selection of a semi-structured interview approach in Section 3.5.2. Discussion is then provided as to how an appropriate interview schedule was conceived.

3.5.1 In-Depth Interviews

According to Merriam (1998), 'in all forms of qualitative research, some and occasionally all of the data are collected through interviews' (p. 71). Merriam also stated that interviewing is necessary when the researcher cannot directly observe behaviour or people's feelings, or when the researcher is interested in past events, such as a sport tourism event which has been held in the past twelve months, as was the case with this research.

Three interview formats exist upon a continuum of interview types (Minichiello, Aroni, Timewell, & Alexander, 1995). These interview types are 1) the structured interview, 2) the semi-structured interview, and 3) the unstructured interview (Jennings, 2001; Merriam, 1998; Minichiello et al., 1995).

At the beginning of the continuum, *structured interviews* were described as 'oral surveys', in which the same standardised, carefully ordered questions are asked of each respondent (Minichiello et al., 1995). At the next level, *semi-structured interviews* utilised a broad research topic to formulate a set of interview questions used to guide the conversation. Such an interview format allowed scope for the researcher to ask probing questions in order to clarify responses (Minichiello et al., 1995). On the final level of the continuum, *unstructured interviews* do without any formal interview schedule, and relied on the social interaction between the interviewer and interviewee to elicit information (Minichiello et al., 1995).

Section 3.5.1 justified the use of in-depth interviews as an appropriate method of data collection for this study. However, the literature established that three types of in-depth interviews exist: structured, semi-structured and unstructured interviews. Section 3.5.2 documents how semi-structured interviews were chosen to be the appropriate interview structure for this study.

3.5.2 Semi-Structured Interviews

In extracting the required data, semi-structured interviews were adopted to examine and explore sponsorship agreements between SMEs and regional sport tourism events. The rationale behind employing semi-structured interviews in this study was that semi-structured interviews possess a distinct advantage due to their ability to elicit detailed information regarding attitudes, opinions, and values of respondents (Jennings, 2001). Given that the research objectives of this study directly or indirectly aimed to explore attitudes, opinions and values of its respondents, it was decided that semi-structured interviews were a suitable data collection technique for this research.

The advantages of semi-structured interviews are outlined in this section and lend justification to their use in this research. The literature stated that semi-structured interviews:

- Are useful when informants cannot be directly observed (Creswell, 1994);
- Allow the researcher some control over the line of questioning (Creswell, 1994);
- Permit detailed information regarding values, opinions and values to be elicited (Jennings, 2001);
- Allow for clarification of responses, along with deeper exploration of discussion issues (Jennings, 2001); and
- Provides a more relaxed interview setting (Jennings, 2001).

Additionally, Guba's (1990) three considerations of ontology, epistemology and methodology (introduced in Section 3.2) assisted in justifying the use of semi-structured interviews for this research into sponsorship agreements. Table 3.3 applied Guba's three considerations to the three forms of interview structures.

Table 3.3: Differences between interview types (source: adapted from Jennings, 2001, p. 163).

	Structured Interviews	**Semi-structured Interviews**	**Unstructured Interviews**
Ontology	Closed world view – universal truths and reality	Multiple realities	Multiple realities
Epistemology	Objective (subjects and study units)	Subjective (participants and phenomenon)	Subjective (participants and phenomenon)
Methodology	Quantitative	Qualitative	Qualitative

As alluded to in Section 3.2, this research is grounded in the interpretive social science paradigm, and therefore assumes an ontological view of multiple realities, in addition to featuring a subjective epistemology between the researcher and the participants. Consequently, the use of a structured interview format was not possible, according to Table 3.3. As such, possible options left were semi-structured or unstructured interviews. Marshall and Rossman (1999) stated that 'a degree of systemisation in questioning may be necessary in, for example, a multisite case study or when many participants are interviewed' (p. 108). Given that this research entailed conducting interviews with multiple event managers and sponsors, a semi-structured interview style was adopted.

When formulating appropriate interview questions, Marshall and Rossman (1999) felt that the methods of data collection should relate to the type of information sought. Consequently, the research objectives of this study provided the foundation for the construction of questions to guide the semi-structured interviews. Topics of inquiry are outlined in Table 3.4.

On all occasions the researcher travelled to a location convenient for the interviewee in order to minimise inconvenience to participants. Each interview was tape-recorded to facilitate the conversational flow of the interviews and to ensure that no important comments were omitted from the collected interview data. Participants' permission to have their interview tape-recorded was sought via the informed consent form, which was mailed to each participant when requesting their participation in the study. Upon completion of each interview, the researcher transcribed recorded data verbatim.

Table 3.4: Interview question topics for the present study.

Event Managers	Business Managers
How the event manager would define sponsorship in their own words	Reasons for providing sponsorship to respective event
Event managers' perception of the key characteristics of a successful sponsorship agreement between an event and a business	Whether the manager had an inclination to provide support to sports or activities in which he/she has a personal interest in
Familiarity of the concept of leveraging	How the manager would define sponsorship in their own words
If the event encourages sponsors to conduct leveraging activities	Familiarity of the concept of leveraging
If the event provides any advice to sponsors as to how they may fully exploit the opportunity	If and how the business utilised leveraging in their sponsorship of the event in question
Attitude held toward the evaluation of sponsorship evaluation	If and how the business evaluated its sponsorship of the event in question
If and how the event evaluated the success of sponsorships as a service to its sponsors	Attitude held toward the evaluation of sponsorship evaluation

Section 3.5.2 has justified the selection of semi-structured interviews as the appropriate interview structure for this research into SME sponsorship of regional sport tourism events. This section also outlined the types of questions asked of participants and how the interviews were conducted. Section 3.6 now discusses the data analysis procedures used in this research.

3.6 Data Analysis

Neuman (2003) described qualitative data as being in the form of 'text, written words, phrases, or symbols describing or representing people, actions, and events in social life' (p. 438), and felt that no single qualitative data analysis approach is widely accepted. To analyse collected interview data, a three-stage process proposed by Miles and Huberman (1994) was adopted for this research. Miles and Huberman's process consisted of 1) data reduction, 2) data display, and 3) conclusion forming and verification.

Miles and Huberman (1994) described the procedures for undertaking this processes of analysis as follows: *data reduction* refers to the process of simplifying and transforming collected data into a manageable form, which is generally by way of textual transcriptions. *Data display* involves the transformation of reduced data into a formation that permits conclusion drawing and action, which in qualitative research is often in the form of extended text. Lastly, *conclusion forming and verification* refers to the researcher 'noting regularities, patterns, explanations, possible configurations, casual flows and propositions' (p. 11), in addition to confirming the validity of meanings emerging from the data through consultation with field notes or consultation with the respective respondent.

Lending further justification to the use of Miles and Huberman's (1994) process of data analysis was the fact that this process was successfully utilised in previous similar research by Arthur (1999). Arthur's doctoral research investigated the corporate decision-making process in the purchasing of sport sponsorship opportunities in Australia.

Section 3.6 outlined the method employed to analyse collected data from interviews with event managers and SME sponsors throughout the course of this research. Section 3.7 goes on to document the pilot study conducted prior to formal data collection.

3.7 Pilot Study

Yin (2003) suggested that the pilot study is the final preparation step prior to formal data collection in a qualitative study, whilst Jennings (2001) felt that if a researcher develops an interview schedule, 'then the schedule has to be tested to ensure that the questions are appropriately framed in order to acquire the required data' (p.152). Given the importance attached to pilot testing in a qualitative study by these researchers, a pilot study was conducted as a precursor to formal data collection commencing.

It was decided to pilot test one case study, which involved interviewing the manager of a sport tourism event within the research area, followed by identifying, approaching and interviewing an SME sponsor of that event. Yin (2003) advocated convenience, access and geographical proximity as being the criteria for selecting the pilot case or cases. Given Yin's suggestion, it was decided to target an event manager known personally, and that was geographically convenient to the researcher. The event manager was contacted initially by telephone and consented to an interview. The interviewee was able to comprehend all questions asked of him, and resulted in good quality data being recorded. Consequently, it was deemed that the event manager interview schedule (refer Appendix A) was acceptable, however it should be acknowledged that the interview schedule had been scrutinised previously by the researcher's supervisor in addition to several other postgraduate students which significantly assisted in constructing a satisfactory interview schedule.

Upon completion of the event manager interview, the event manager was asked which one of the event's sponsors would be the most receptive to an invitation to participate in the research. The event manager obliged and the identified sponsor was posted a mail package requesting their participation in this study, to which they agreed. The interview was conducted with the interviewee being able to comprehend and respond receptively to all questions asked of him. However, this interview generated significantly less data in terms of number of pages of interview transcript compared with that of the event manager. Upon reviewing both transcripts, it was found that the sponsor was much more succinct in his responses than those of the event manager, who tended to 'pad out' his responses by occasionally repeating himself and frequently offering example scenarios. As such, it was conceded that the sponsor interview schedule (refer Appendix B) was acceptable. However, following transcription of this interview, a number of responses were identified that could have generated higher quality data if the researcher had been more studious in asking explanatory or probing questions. Neuman (2003) stated that probes such as, *'can you tell me more about that'?*, *'What do you mean by that'?* and *'how do you mean'?* are effective means of clarifying ambiguous or inaccurate interview responses.

In summary, the pilot case study revealed no major flaws in the proposed interview schedules and they were subsequently accepted to guide the formal data collection interviews. Arising from the pilot case study was a need for the researcher to be more diligent in listening to the finer detail of interviewee's responses and be more scrupulous in asking probe questions in order to clarify incomplete or inaccurate answers.

Section 3.7 has outlined the pilot study conducted as a precursor to the commencement of data collection. Section 3.8 presents the final area relevant to the methodological processes employed to conduct this research, 'trustworthiness' of the research.

3.8 'Trustworthiness' of the Research

An important concern when conducting research is to produce valid and reliable (or 'trustworthy') knowledge through ethical and academically rigourous means (Merriam, 1998). Patton (2002) felt that rigour of qualitative research 'has to do with the quality of the observations made by an evaluator' (p. 575) and the ability of the researcher to maintain an objective perception of the phenomenon under investigation at all times.

Merriam (1998, p. 204-205) proposed six strategies that may enhance the trustworthiness of a piece of qualitative research. These strategies were:

1. **Triangulation:** The use of multiple researchers, multiple data sources or mixed methods, designed to confirm the emerging research findings.
2. **Member checks:** Returning data and initial analyses to the people they were derived from and asking them if the results represent a fair and reasonable account of the phenomenon.

3. **Long-term observation:** Gathering data over a long period of time or through repeated observations of a phenomenon to increase the validity of the findings.

4. **Peer examination:** Having colleagues scrutinise the findings as they emerge.

5. **Participatory or collaborative modes of research:** Involving participants in the entire process of the study, from conception right through to the writing of the findings.

6. **Acknowledging researcher bias:** Clarifying the researcher's assumptions, ontological and epistemological stances from the very beginning of the research.

Member checking and acknowledging researcher bias were strategies employed to enhance the internal validity of this study. Lincoln and Guba (1985) advocated member checking as a process,

> Whereby data, analytic categories, interpretations, and conclusions are tested with members of those stakeholding groups from whom the data were originally collected, is the most crucial technique for establishing credibility…it provides the respondent the opportunity to volunteer additional information; indeed the act of 'playing back' may stimulate the respondent to recall additional things that were not mentioned the first time around (p. 314).

Once interviews were transcribed verbatim, transcriptions were returned to the participant for the purpose of having them confirm that the transcript was an accurate reflection of their views and value, and also to offer them an opportunity to add information or withdraw statements they did not wish to have included in the research. The ontological stance of the researcher was acknowledged in Section 3.2 in that the researcher believed that differing explanations for the phenomena under investigation may exist as opposed to one universal explanation. Epistemologically, the researcher accepted that this research may not be able to be replicated and the same results obtained by another researcher, owing to the interaction between the researcher and interviewer. In some instances, interviewees were known personally to the researcher and as such may not offer such open and detailed responses to other investigators.

Section 3.8 has discussed the strategy adopted to establish trustworthiness of this research, which involved member checks and the acknowledgement of possible researcher bias, as advocated by Merriam (1998).

3.9 Chapter Summary

This chapter has described the construction of the methodology designed to thoroughly examine and explore sponsorship agreements between SMEs and regional sport tourism events.

Chapter Three justified the use of qualitative, multiple case studies as the research strategy, and semi-structured interviews as the data collection tool. The geographical research area was also identified within this chapter, along with the process for selecting appropriate events and sponsors to approach for participation in this research. The pilot study conducted prior to formal data collection was documented, as were strategies adopted to establish trustworthiness of the research.

Chapter Four now presents the results obtained from the interviews conducted with sponsors and event managers.

CHAPTER FOUR

RESULTS

4.1 Introduction and Description of Cases

Chapter Three outlined the methodological approach constructed to conduct this research. Chapter Four now presents the results of in-depth interviews conducted with the event managers of purposively selected events, and with a respective sponsor of each event. Yin (2003) stated that research involving multiple case studies are 'usually presented as separate chapters or sections about each of the cases singly', as is the case with this research. Consequently, each case study is presented separately for the purpose of this chapter. Section 4.1 provides background information for each case, while Section 4.2 onwards presents the results of each case study's in-depth interviews.

As mentioned in Chapter Three, it was initially proposed that six case studies would be undertaken to form the basis for this study, or until the point of literal replication was reached (Yin, 2003). After five case studies had been investigated, no significant new data was being generated and the researcher elected to cease data collection at that point. Table 4.1 provides a summary of the five case studies that formed the data sources for this study.

Table 4.1: Summary of case studies.

Case Number	Event	Sponsor
1	Horse racing carnival	Car dealership
2	Masters Games	Registered club
3	Triathlon	Real estate agent
4	Ocean swim	Bus company
5	Triathlon	Financial institution

4.1.1 Case Study Number One

Case study one centred on a one-day provincial horse racing carnival. The carnival was the most prestigious event of its kind within the research area and attracted some 9,000 patrons for the 2004 event. A total of 33 businesses provided cash and in-kind sponsorship to this event. The interview in this case was conducted with the secretary of the turf club. This person was employed by the turf club on a full-time basis and held responsibility for sourcing and managing sponsorships for all the club's events.

The sponsor targeted for inclusion in this case was a car dealership in the same town as the horse racing carnival. This business dealt in prestige motor vehicles and has been involved in this event as a sponsor for approximately ten years. Less than twenty people were employed by this car dealership, and was therefore classified as a small business. In this case, the interview was carried out with the owner of the dealership. This sponsorship consisted of a cash contribution with a value in the vicinity of AU$2,000.

4.1.2 Case Study Number Two

A bi-annual event for older athletes formed the basis for case study two. The event has been held twice previously and encompasses a broad range of sports over a period of four days, which has historically attracted approximately 2,000 participants plus their entourage to the host community. Eight sponsorship opportunities associated with the games provided the funding needed to stage the event, one of which was the *major* (naming rights) sponsor whom provided a significantly higher amount of cash sponsorship than the remaining seven sponsors. The event was organised and run by a paid event coordinator employed full-time by the local council, who was also the person interviewed for the purpose of this case study.

In addition to the eight core sponsors of the games, numerous other minor sponsors were involved in the event. Each activity under the Masters Games umbrella was organised and run by the local organisation for each respective sport, for example cricket was run by the [name of town] cricket club. Each individual sport was required to pay the games organisers a AU$600 'entry fee'. In many cases this money was provided by a sponsor sourced by the organisation running a respective activity. In return the sponsor received access to some of the commercially exploitable rights to that sport.

The researcher was able to interview the general manager of the major sponsor of the games. This business was a registered club, which featured a wide range of facilities for its members and guests, including several bars, gaming facilities, a bistro and numerous function rooms. The club employed approximately 120 people, and was classified as a medium business. This sponsorship consisted of a cash contribution to the Masters Games in the vicinity of AU$20,000 and was by far the most expensive sponsorship of all the case studies investigated in this research.

4.1.3 Case Study Number Three

Case study three focused on a triathlon event held in a small coastal town, in which participants compete in a swim, cycle, run combination. The event was organised and run by a community-based triathlon club, in which all persons involved in the coordination of this event were unpaid volunteers. The triathlon was conducted for the first time in 2004 and is now pencilled in as an annual event. The inaugural event attracted approximately 250 competitors, including a former Olympic swimming gold medallist. There was a strong emphasis on community involvement, with a secondary objective of developing the sport by encouraging people to simply 'have a go'. The person interviewed in this instance was the president of the triathlon club, who was also responsible for managing the event's sponsorships.

One local business was the major sponsor of this event. It provided cash sponsorship to fund the staging of the triathlon. Approximately ten other local businesses provided sponsorship to the event by way of small cash contributions, or in-kind support relevant to the event.

The sponsor investigated in case study number three was the major sponsor of the triathlon, and was the local branch of a real estate chain. Although this business was a subsidiary of a franchise, the sponsorship funds originated from the assets of the actual agency in the host town, thus the business was deemed suitable for inclusion in the research. The real estate agency employed approximately seven people, and therefore was classified as a small business. The principal of the business was interviewed during the course of this research. This sponsorship consisted of a cash contribution to the triathlon with a value of around AU$1,500.

4.1.4 Case Study Number Four

An ocean swim classic formed the foundation for case study number four. This event was an annual event held in the waters off a coastal town. The inaugural swim classic was held in 1992, and in 2005 attracted nearly 1,000 competitors ranging in age from 14 to 76 years including many state, national and international swimming champions. This event was organised by a local swimming club, in which all persons involved in the running of the event did so in a voluntary capacity.

This ocean swim has a successful sponsorship history, consistently attracting significant amounts of cash and product sponsorship each year owing to the event's charitable nature. All profits generated by the event were distributed to local charities such as the local hospital, rescue groups, surf lifesaving club, nursing homes and schools. Sponsorships were categorised according to a three-tiered format (gold, silver and bronze), with benefits on offer proportional to the value of support provided to the event.

A bus company was the business selected for participation in this case study. Bus transport of competitors from the registration precinct to the race start venue was the form of sponsorship provided by this business to the ocean swim classic. This arrangement has been in place since the event was conceptualised. This business primarily provides school bus services and services linking major towns within the research area. This company employed a varying number of staff according to business needs, however always employed more than twenty, but less than 200 persons which meant it was classified as a medium sized business. The interview in this instance was conducted with the general manager of the company, who was responsible for overseeing this business' sponsorships. The sponsorship contribution made to the ocean swim classic was in the form of provision of buses and drivers to transport athletes to the race start venue, free of charge. This was the least expensive sponsorship of all the case studies pursued in this research.

4.1.5 Case Study Number Five

A triathlon staged annually in a small coastal village underpinned case study number five. The event was conducted by the local athletics club by unpaid volunteers. The triathlon has been held for a number of years, and owing to the small size of the host village, many local businesses contributed small amounts of cash sponsorship or product support. The event is highly informal, with the primary aim of the triathlon being to attract visitors to the village and stimulate business during a quiet time of the year. The event consistently attracts in excess of one hundred competitors, many of whom travel considerable distances within the research area to compete.

The major sponsor of the triathlon consented to be interviewed for this case study. The business was a small chain of community credit unions. In this instance, the credit union chain as a whole provided the funds required to stage the event, and was the naming rights sponsor. As the chain employed less than 200 persons at the time of the most recent running of the triathlon, the business was classified as a medium sized enterprise. The interview was conducted with the manager of the credit union branch in the host town, who was the primary instigator and caretaker of this sponsorship. A cash contribution of less than AU$1,000 was the credit union's sponsorship input to the triathlon.

4.2 In-Depth Interview Results

This section presents the analysed qualitative data emerging from in-depth interviews conducted with event managers and sponsors of regional sport tourism events within the research area. The results are presented utilising the five research objectives (refer Chapter One) as subheadings within each case study. Each participant interviewed during this study was assigned a two-character identifier. The first character was either S or E, with S signifying that person was a sponsor and E signifying an event manager. The second character identified the participant's case study number. Thus the sponsor of case number one was assigned the identifier S1, and the event manager from case number two was assigned the identifier E2, and so on. Participants are referred to using this identifier throughout the following chapters.

4.2.1 Case Study One Results (Horse Racing Carnival/Car Dealership)

Sponsor and Event Manager's Perceptions of what constitutes 'sponsorship'

When asked to define the term 'sponsorship', S1 initially responded jovially, defining sponsorship as *'a waste of money'*. However, after considering the question further he responded more seriously, defining sponsorship as *'business charity'*, and explained that sponsorship in general provided his business with a vehicle to give something back to the local community. E1 felt that the definition of sponsorship is rather subjective. He defined sponsorship as:

> *'Showing your support for a particular event or sport by lending your name to that event and being prepared to pay for the privilege of lending your name, having your name on that event'.*

E1 explained that his club was generally a recipient of sponsorship support, and therefore has a responsibility to ensure that sponsors are receiving value for their investment. Cash sponsorship was viewed as vitally important to the success of the racing carnival, and E1 felt that the turf club was *'fighting a constant battle'* to ensure that sufficient sponsorship funds are available, and that sponsors were receiving benefits proportionate to the size of their investment.

Business' Reason for Sponsoring this Event

S1 cited a variety of reasons for sponsoring the racing carnival. Signage and exposure in front of a large crowd of people in the business' local community provided the initial attraction for providing sponsorship when the business first became a sponsor in 1995. At this time, S1 purchased the naming rights to one race during the carnival, which he claimed generated substantial publicity for the business. S1 also stated that this event carried with it a lot of prestige in the local region and it was *'just nice to be involved'*.

The opportunity to provide hospitality to staff, clients and executive members of the motor vehicle brand the dealership trades in was also cited by S1 as an influential factor in electing to sponsor the racing carnival. Given that the local council gazetted a half-day public holiday in the host town for the carnival, S1 believed that this gave him an excellent opportunity to *'wine and dine'* his staff members. *'Giving back to the community'* was also cited by S1 as a reason for sponsoring the racing carnival.

Therefore, the primary reasons why this car dealership sponsored the racing carnival were:
- To gain exposure and publicity;

- Offer corporate hospitality to staff and clients; and
- To give back to the local community.

If and How Leveraging Occurred within this Sponsorship

When asked if any promotional activities were conducted with the aim of enhancing return on the sponsorship investment, S1 explained that his business did little to leverage the sponsorship. The only activity cited was that of conducting some informal networking amongst other business associates whilst at the actual carnival. In summary, no attempt was made by this business to leverage this sponsorship.

E1 stated that he did encourage sponsors to leverage their investments by providing advice to sponsors (particularly new sponsors) as to how they may capitalise on their sponsorship. The most frequently dispensed advice to sponsors pertained to corporate hospitality. The following is a quote from E1 who gave an example of the kind of leveraging advice given to sponsors:

> *'Most of them don't realise they can put banners and signs up so we say, go and get a banner made up and put it on the fence so people can see. Your name's on a race, once that race is run there's a chance people will forget, but if you've got the banner up there and someone sees it ten or fifteen times during the day it will stick, that that name is there. So we encourage that type of stuff'* (E1).

E1 stated that he frequently dispensed such advice in order to protect the viability of future sponsorships. It was explained that many of the carnival's sponsors were very casual about sponsorships, *'they just want to be involved in the day'*. However, E1 maintained that he is very proactive in encouraging its sponsors to leverage their investment so that when the time comes to renew the agreement, sponsors are less likely to question the value of providing sponsorship to the carnival. Therefore, to encourage sponsorship leveraging, the turf club advised its sponsors to:

- Place signage at the event; and
- Invest funds in providing hospitality to their most valued clients.

Sponsor and Event Manager's Attitudes towards & Practices of Sponsorship Evaluation

S1 did not attempt to measure the success of its sponsorship of the racing carnival. S1 felt that doing so would be very difficult and was unsure if any effective techniques for sponsorship evaluation existed. The only feedback measure S1 took into consideration was *'the amount of talk you get over the counter in the weeks after'*. However, S1 noted that if only 1,500 people attended the following year's carnival as opposed to the 9,000 that usually attend, then the dealership would reconsider its sponsorship of the event.

E1 also did not conduct any formal evaluation of sponsorships for its events. E1 justified not evaluating because he felt that the feedback may not always be positive and that the turf club may not be able to cater for the needs and wants of sponsors:

> *'We've never sent out formal surveys saying, 'are you happy with this bla bla bla...' possibly because we're scared of the answers we're going to get. We might start getting demands that we can't meet or are too difficult to do on the day'* (E1).

However, E1 explained that some informal evaluation was conducted by way of casual conversation with sponsors in the weeks after the carnival. It was also noted that the time it takes for a sponsor '*to pay the bill*' was an indication of a sponsor's satisfaction level, '*if you get the invoice paid within a month you know they're pretty happy. If you have to start chasing the money you know there's usually a reason for it*'.

E1 stated that he provided no written feedback to sponsors with regard to the impact of their sponsorship of the racing carnival.

How the Sponsorship was Initiated

According to S1, this relationship began through a business associate of his, who was a member of the turf club committee at the time. The turf club committee member issued a request to S1 for sponsorship of the racing carnival in exchange for signage on the finish post. The request was accepted and S1 stated that he enjoyed the experience, and the relationship grew from this point. It can therefore be said that this sponsorship began through a personal contact of S1.

In providing sponsorship to the racing carnival, S1 had no specific objective it wished to achieve through the arrangement, other than gaining exposure via signage at the racetrack. S1 stated that his business had no formal process in place in deciding which causes to provide sponsorship to, other than '*trial and error ... it's what you think is best for you*'.

There was a degree of formality in the way the turf club managed this relationship in that pre-determined sponsorship packages are available for purchase by businesses, in which specific benefits were available and catalogued. Such benefits included racetrack signage, advertising in race programs, complementary tickets, and hospitality opportunities. E1 stated that keeping sponsors involved and allowing sufficient lead-time was important in maintaining sponsorship relationships:

> *'It's also keeping them involved in the lead-up. For me it's not like ringing them up two weeks before the event and saying, 'hey, are you sponsoring again?', 'yep, no worries'. We contact them five months before the event and propose the package to them. In the lead-up I have four or five conversations with them to make sure they're happy with how things are going, that we haven't missed anything along the way. Are there any other things that they want to do that we can help them with as far as their profile on the day? It's making them feel special as well I suppose, that they are a major part of the day. The letter that I send out, it says, 'This is [the town's] biggest social event of the year, we would like you and your business to remain an integral part of the success of the day'. They like to feel they have part of the ownership of that day'* (E1).

However, E1 did note that when he is attempting to sell a sponsorship package, there is no set way in which he deals with people, *'apart from the actual proposals we send out, I sort of wing it mostly'*.

To conclude, this relationship was initiated through a personal contact of the car dealership owner. There was no desire by the car dealership to achieve any specific objective through the sponsorship and in general, the dealership handled its sponsorships with a low degree of formality. The turf club however, managed its sponsorships with a higher degree of formality in the form of predetermined sponsorship packages that were available for purchase.

4.2.2 Case Study Two Results (Masters Games/Registered Club)

Sponsor and Event Manager's Perceptions of what constitutes 'sponsorship'

'An amount of money or in-kind service that we give to an organisation and in return they give us recognition', was how S2 defined sponsorship. Return on investment and opportunities to leverage business back through the doors of the club were two other characteristics seen to be important in sponsorship by this business. Sponsorship for philanthropic purposes was not engaged in by this business, *'we don't just hand money over, like 'here's $5,000 now go away'. They need to give us something back'* (S2).

E2 saw sponsorship as an unequal relationship, with the major beneficiary being the sponsored party. He defined sponsorship as:

> *'An agreement with a mutual benefit to both. But the benefit's definitely ours. We hold the cards but you don't be blasé about it because you want them to come back'* (E2).

E2 named a condition he described as *'a political level of comfort'* with the event on the part of sponsors as also being an important factor in a successful sponsorship. In explaining this condition, alignment was made with a risk a sponsor takes in underwriting an event, which is the possibility of losing money through the arrangement, but being comfortable with that risk due to the sponsor's intrinsic interest in sport, *'generosity doesn't play a part, but it probably does a little bit'* (E2). Delivering intangible benefits, such as the registered club observing people dancing and enjoying the event, were another factor contributing to a successful sponsorship according to E2.

Business' Reason for Sponsoring this Event

A number of reasons were cited by S2 for providing sponsorship to the Masters Games. The primary reason was to encourage sport and *'good fellowship amongst the members and non-members'*. The potential to gain future members and status within the local community were other reasons for underwriting the event, as was the potential for attracting media attention for the club through the event.

Reasons stimulated by external forces such as government legislation were also behind the decision to sponsor this event. As the business generated in excess of AU$1 million in poker machine revenue, it was required by law to spend a percentage of this revenue on community causes such as under-privileged children and sporting organisations.

The potential for leveraging significant amounts of business back into the club was also cited as a reason for sponsoring this event. As the event held three functions which included a pre-games welcome dinner and presentation evening, the club was filled to capacity three times in four days, delivering a significant amount of business to the club.

Therefore, the reasons driving the club's decision to sponsor the Masters Games were:

- To encourage sport and good fellowship;
- Potential for gaining future members;
- To enhance business image within local community;
- To gain media exposure;
- External forces (government legislation); and
- Potential for leveraging business.

If and How Leveraging Occurred within this Sponsorship

S2 stated that the club did not make any attempt to leverage the sponsorship. Additionally, S2 stated that no attempt was made to leverage the sponsorship through media advertising or in-house promotions associated with the event.

With regard to providing advice to sponsors as to how they may capitalise on their investment, E2 did not provide any such advice in an up-front manner, *'we don't tell them how to do their business'*. However, if a sponsor wished to conduct a promotion or activity to enhance return on investment, E2 stated that he would do everything within his powers to facilitate such leveraging activities, *'it's certainly our responsibility to help them'*.

In summary, neither party stated that any attempt was made to leverage this sponsorship. However, E2 did state that his event was obligated to assist sponsors where necessary, in leveraging their sponsorships and in doing this provides information pertaining to how they may conduct a leveraging activity.

Sponsor and Event Manager's Attitudes towards & Practices of Sponsorship Evaluation

S2 stated that following the running of the Masters Games, an evaluation of the sponsorship was conducted, which centred on bottom-line impact. A form of cost-benefit analysis was conducted in measuring the success of the sponsorship, *'what we did was over a week, took all our trading results and measured that against the* [dollar amount of] *sponsorship we gave'*. S2 did note that evaluating the sponsorship and quantifying the success in dollar terms was difficult to achieve. It was also mentioned by S2 that media exposure was monitored, albeit it with a low degree of importance.

In order to ascertain whether the sponsors of the event were satisfied with the outcomes of their investments in the Masters Games, E2 conducted both quantitative and qualitative inquiries into the matter. The quantitative evaluation involved a written survey administered to the sponsors, in which seven broad open-ended questions pertaining to sponsors' level of contentment with the delivery of the sponsorship package were posed. E2 remarked that it was often difficult to have the survey completed by and returned from the sponsors, except in instances where a sponsor was dissatisfied:

> *'It's a formal survey that we struggle to get back from them sometimes. That usually means they're happy. If they're angry, they rip us out* [criticise them]*'* (E2).

Qualitative evaluation was conducted at a post-event breakfast, which was held to thank the event's sponsors. Evaluation took place during casual conversation with sponsors:

> *'We usually have a post-event function with the sponsors which is usually just a breakfast or something and we ask them very candid questions, happy, sad, good, bad, happy, why, how come?'* (E2).

It was noted by E2 that the qualitative evaluation process proved to be more effective in eliciting sponsor satisfaction rates, *'you tend to get the good oil from the verbal process, and we usually do'*.

Feedback to sponsors following the games was provided in the form of a generic report presented to the local council. As part of this report, the results of a post-event competitor survey were included, in which a sponsor recall test indicated recall rates by competitors of which businesses sponsored the event.

To summarise, both parties evaluated the sponsorship of the Masters Games event in a fairly formal manner. Methods of sponsorship evaluation employed in this instance were cost-benefit analysis, quantitative survey, and informal qualitative interviewing.

How the Sponsorship was Initiated

This sponsorship agreement came about as a result of the Masters Games organisers approaching the registered club and requesting sponsorship for the 2001 event. E2 stated that the club was identified as a potential sponsor on logistical grounds as well as the club's past history of providing cash sponsorships to events and sporting associations in the local area. E2 felt that the social club was the only venue in the host town capable of accommodating the number of competitors and entourage expected to attend the Masters Games functions (welcome dinner, registrations and farewell dinner). The event organisers noted that the sponsorship could be a natural success as there was potential for the club to leverage significant amounts of business from the sponsorship.

Additionally, the club had objectives pertaining to media exposure, encouraging sport, increased sales, and being seen as a responsible corporate citizen within the local community that it wished to achieve, while the event relied on the sponsorship funds to make it solvent.

4.2.3 Case Study Three Results (Triathlon/Real Estate Agency)

Sponsor and Event Manager's Perceptions of what constitutes 'sponsorship'

S3 viewed sponsorship primarily as a means for a business to give something back to its local community, whilst also achieving exposure and recognition of the business for doing so:

> *'Sponsorship is putting something back into the community that gives us so much, but in doing that you're also achieving awareness of your brand, whichever it whether it be real estate or a bottleshop or whatever...sponsorship is about putting something back into the*

community that services you on a daily basis...but we're also trying to seek awareness out of that as well' (S3).

Sponsorship was not seen by S3 as philanthropy, and did not allocate sponsorship funds to any cause unless the business was to receive some form of direct benefit:

'You can't just go sponsoring 'willy-nilly' for anything...unless it's got a direct impact on or an impact on our business future-wise, we wouldn't go there' (S3).

Sponsorship was defined by E3 as simply, 'somebody that comes to you and gives you cash or product to run an event for a club or organisation'.

Business' Reason for Sponsoring this Event

The sponsor of case number three was unique within this study in that S3 actually conceptualised the triathlon. This business (a real estate agency) wished to attract visitors to the host town during a renowned period of slow business. S3 saw a triathlon as an ideal event to achieve this objective and made contact with a triathlon club in the region, who agreed to organise and run the event, with the real estate agency as the major sponsor.

S3 predicted that staging a triathlon would have a direct impact on his business as out-of-town visitors would need to rent accommodation facilities managed by the business. Additionally, S3 wished to achieve awareness of the town as a tourist destination, which would also positively impact upon the business. S3 felt that if any of the triathlon's competitors did return to the town for a holiday, they would most likely source accommodation through his business:

'Through the 250 people we got here last year, each one of them, if they ever came back, I'm pretty confident our name would be in their heads, if they wanted to come back for a holiday' (S3).

S3 also noted that there was potential for the triathlon to entice people looking to move to the coast for a sea change, to consider this town for relocation. Naturally, if this did come to fruition, it could positively impact upon this real estate agency, as S3 explained, *'I've only got to sell one house and I've covered my sponsorship of the triathlon for three or four years'*. Media exposure of the business' name and logo were also cited as a reason for undertaking this sponsorship.

A reason pertaining to obtaining personal satisfaction in giving back to the community was also cited by S3 for sponsoring the triathlon:

'By us sponsoring this event, it gives me great pleasure that Tammy and Kenny [owners of café where interview took place] *here will be flat out on the Sunday morning or the Saturday*

> *morning because of the extra 100 people coming into the town. So they know without our sponsorship of this or our organisation, they know they wouldn't be getting that clientele in the town, so to me it gives me a great deal of satisfaction in knowing these businesses, that we're supporting the town and supporting them'* (S3).

To summarise, the reasons why this business sponsors the triathlon were:

- To attract visitors to its town and stimulate business during a slow time of year;
- To achieve increased sales;
- To increase awareness of the business;
- Gain media exposure; and
- To give back to the local community.

If and How Leveraging Occurred within this Sponsorship

Both parties indicated that they made no attempt to leverage this sponsorship. However, it was noted by the researcher that the real estate agency did have a section on the event entry form that suggested that competitors looking for accommodation should contact the real estate agency.

E3 stated that the triathlon club provided no advice to the sponsor as to how they might enhance their return on investment.

To conclude, there was no evidence to suggest that either party in this case made any attempt to leverage this sponsorship.

Sponsor and Event Manager's Attitudes towards & Practices of Sponsorship Evaluation

Both parties stated that the sponsorship was evaluated following the running of the triathlon. S3 commented that he assessed the success of the sponsorship in terms of the number of accommodation properties that were rented out on the weekend of the race. S3 declared the sponsorship a success in the short term owing to the fact that all accommodation properties under his business' management were full, and that he managed to fill twenty other properties managed by other real estate agents in the town, owing to demand from competitors in the triathlon:

> *'We evaluated how it had an impact on our business. In doing that we looked at all our accommodation facilities, which were full that weekend. We even approached the other agencies and did a deal with them because everyone was ringing us obviously in regard to this, and started renting out their accommodation and we filled the others [other properties*

managed by real estate agencies in the town] up too, so in our opinion it had a great impact on our business in the short term' (S3).

When asked if evaluation was an important part of maintaining the sponsorship of the triathlon, S3 felt that it was important but also remarked that he had taken the process of evaluation in a rather casual manner and that the business was going to look into implementing a more formal process of evaluation for the following year's event.

E3 stated that the sponsorship was evaluated on his part via a meeting with the sponsor in the weeks following the event. However, when probed about this meeting E3 was unable to recall what aspects of the sponsorship were evaluated.

In summing up, the success of this sponsorship was evaluated primarily by the sponsor. In doing so, the direct impact on sales (accommodation properties occupied) was the indicator used to determine if the sponsorship was a success or not.

How the Sponsorship was Initiated

This sponsorship was initialised through a request from the real estate agency to the region's triathlon club to run an event, which was designed to achieve objectives set out by the real estate agency. E3 described the request as a golden opportunity for his triathlon club as a sponsor was knocking on his door as opposed to the club having to go out and source sponsorship itself, *'it's every race director's dream. They basically said, tell us what you need and we will come through with it'* (E3).

The sponsorship arrangement was of an informal nature, *'it was a handshake sort of agreement'*, as E3 noted. The lack of leveraging and the small-scale evaluation of the sponsorship was also testament to the informality of the relationship.

4.2.4 Case Study Four Results (Ocean Swim/Bus Company)

Sponsor and Event Manager's Perceptions of what constitutes 'sponsorship'

E4 defined sponsorship as *'giving money to assist a promotion, you don't get as much out of it as you put into it'*. Throughout the course of this interview, it became apparent that this event viewed sponsorship as a somewhat altruistic practice. At one point, E4 referred to the sponsorship provided by the naming rights sponsor as a donation, *'it's just another extremely generous donation by the [sponsor]'*. E4 was also of the opinion that none of the sponsors of the ocean swim classic had an interest on return on investment or achieving corporate objectives through their involvement with the event, *'they just want to be part of it'* (E4).

S4, who provided in-kind sponsorship to the ocean swim classic in the form of buses to transport competitors to the race start venue viewed sponsorship in a purely philanthropic manner. He defined sponsorship as, '*giving something to an event, we don't expect much out of it at the end of the day regardless of what it is*' (S4).

Business' Reason for Sponsoring this Event

S4 stated that in the business providing sponsorship to the ocean swim classic, '*there was no real reason for it, we just did it*'. Reasons pertaining to being approached for the sponsorship by a member of the event organising committee, and being seen as doing something for the community were offered in justifying the sponsorship.

To summarise, the reasons why the bus company provided sponsorship to the ocean swim classic were:

- Because the person who requested the sponsorship was a known to the business; and
- To give back to the local community.

If and How Leveraging Occurred within this Sponsorship

S4 offered no evidence whatsoever in this instance that suggested that any attempt was made to leverage this sponsorship. When asked if any promotions associated with this sponsorship were conducted, S4 explained that his company did not feel the need to do so, '*we're not in-your-face sort of people*'.

A similar response was offered by E4, who explained that his event did not offer its sponsors any advice as to how they may enhance their return on investment. E4 felt that businesses sponsor the ocean swim classic more for community involvement purposes as opposed to bottom-line objectives, '*they know what they're in for, they just want to be part of it*' (E4).

Given the responses obtained from these two participants, it can be concluded that leveraging did not occur in this sponsorship relationship between the bus company and the ocean swim classic.

Sponsor and Event Manager's Attitudes towards & Practices of Sponsorship Evaluation

Throughout the interviews conducted with S4 and E4, it became clear that evaluation of this sponsorship did not take place. S4 explained that there was no point in evaluating the sponsorship given the informal nature of the sponsorship and the value of support his company offered, '*the only thing I ask from them is a couple of t-shirts*' (S4).

E4 stated that no attempt was made to evaluate any of the sponsorships associated with the ocean swim classic. He explained that all the sponsors, to his knowledge were satisfied with being associated with an event that gives away significant amounts of money to charitable causes in the local area, in addition to the exposure sponsors receive in the local media and on event merchandise (such as t-shirts, entry forms and venue signage). E4 also stated that no formal feedback was provided to sponsors regarding their involvement in the event. However, sponsors were invited to a function held in the weeks after the event during which monies raised were distributed to selected charities, and sponsors formally thanked for their contribution and involvement.

To summarise this section, no evaluation of this sponsorship relationship took place, and in both instances evaluation of sponsorships by both the sponsor and event manager was viewed to be unnecessary.

How the Sponsorship was Initiated

According to S4, this sponsorship was initiated following a letter from the organising body of the ocean swim classic, requesting in-kind sponsorship from the business. As the individual who signed the letter was known personally by S4, the bus company agreed to the request primarily owing to this personal contact.

Both parties described this sponsorship as being very informal. S4 described the level of formality on a scale out of ten, as being around 'one'. E4 explained that all sponsorships associated with the ocean swim classic were on an informal basis. He described the relationship with the event's naming rights sponsor (who provided the most significant amount of cash sponsorship) as being '*a handshake agreement*'.

Therefore, it can be summarised that this sponsorship came to fruition though a personal contact, and that the relationship was of a highly informal nature, as evidenced by the fact that no attempt was made to leverage or evaluate the sponsorship.

4.2.5 Case Study Five Results (Triathlon/Financial Institution)

Sponsor and Event Manager's Perceptions of what constitutes 'sponsorship'

S5 viewed sponsorship as providing support to an event or organisation, with a minor benefit to the sponsor. He defined sponsorship as:

> '*Providing support to an event or organisation that would otherwise struggle without that support...obviously there has to be some sort of benefit [to the sponsor] as far as promotion goes*' (S5).

E5 saw sponsorship as 'a necessary thing…it gives people access to prizes they normally wouldn't get'. He felt that the businesses in the host town sponsored the triathlon 'because it's a small community here…they don't like to say no'. However, E5 also stated that the sponsors 'generally don't have a big interest in it [the triathlon]'. It was also remarked that the triathlon did not offer a great range of benefits to its sponsors, 'no real benefits, we don't offer them anything, just exposure. Basically signage…nobody really has a big enough stake in the event'.

Business' Reason for Sponsoring this Event

S5 cited two primary reasons why the credit union sponsored the triathlon. S5 stressed throughout the interview that the business was highly focused on the community which it services, and that sponsoring the triathlon was an opportunity to assist a community-based sporting organisation to achieve something. S5 explained the sponsorship of the triathlon in stating:

> *'It's also supporting a small, local sporting group, that is achieving a rather significant event…for a small organisation with limited resources to be able to achieve that and have an event go on for that long is a pretty big achievement and it's nice to think that an organisation like ourselves can help a small group like that to achieve a recognised event'* (S5).

The triathlon attracted a significant number of competitors from outside the local community. This feature of the triathlon was seen by S5 as a potential means to obtain exposure to a wider audience outside of the local community as it may sow the seeds for future business as S5 explained, '*it just brings us to the focus of those people because one day they we might be there* [in a visitor's home town] *or one day they might move up here, so that brings us to their attention*'.

Therefore, the reasons why the credit union sponsored the triathlon in case number five were:

- To support a local community organisation; and
- To obtain exposure from an audience outside the local community.

If and How Leveraging Occurred within this Sponsorship

S5 stated that no promotions associated with the triathlon sponsorship were conducted. He felt that this was the responsibility of the triathlon organisers, '*they take care of all the organisation, they send out the entry forms obviously with our logo on it*'. S5 explained that the credit union's sponsorship of the triathlon was promoted by the fact that it owned the naming rights to the triathlon, and by placing event products in the branch during the lead up to the event, '*we'll put a poster up in the branch, we'll have entry forms in the branch to promote it*' (S5).

S5 stated that no promotions associated with the sponsorship were conducted in the local media, however he was looking to conduct some *'fun and games promotion'* in the local newspaper for the 2005 event. S5 also mentioned that he personally attended the presentation ceremony to award prizes to the winners of the triathlon.

The fact that the triathlon has never struggled to attract competitors was offered by S5 as a reason for not attempting to leverage the sponsorship, *'they haven't really had a problem in the past and the number of competitors is growing each year...how big they want it to get being a small club, they don't want it to get too much out of control'* (S5).

E5 stated that he did offer some minor advice to a couple of local businesses that sponsored the 2004 triathlon as to how they may leverage business from their sponsorship:

> *'The café wasn't going to be open when the triathlon was on, so we told them that the triathlon is going to be on at this time, and they opened those hours to cater for it. So they got a direct benefit straight out of it'* (E5).

However, E5 stated that there was no advice offered to the credit union as to how they may capitalise on their sponsorship investment.

To summarise this section, leveraging of the credit union's sponsorship of the triathlon did occur in a minor and indirect sense, owing to the credit union's efforts in placing promotional material in the branch office. E5 however, did not provide any advice to the credit union as to how it may leverage business from its investment.

Sponsor and Event Manager's Attitudes towards & Practices of Sponsorship Evaluation

S5 stated that he did conduct an evaluation of the credit union's sponsorship of the triathlon. In doing this, S5 remarked that the purpose of conducting the evaluation was aimed more at making the process of implementing the following year's sponsorship easier, *'I don't have to, but I do just for their benefit* [central administration department of the credit union] *just so that it's not so hard next year'*. Additionally, S5 felt that because this was the most expensive sponsorship in the town, he was obliged to conduct an evaluation of the sponsorship for the credit union's central administration department:

> *'I'm not obliged to, but I do. I provide some feedback because it is [the town's] largest sponsorship and I think that I should have to provide some justification for the expense. Even though it's not in dollars, I do like to put something on paper for them'* (S5).

The process of conducting this evaluation involved collecting editorials written about the triathlon (in which the credit union was mentioned) in addition to a meeting with the organisers of the triathlon, '*I'll talk to them and ask them how many competitors were there and where did they come from, that sort of stuff just so I can get a general idea of what sort of exposure we got, what areas and what we can do different next year*' (S5). In justifying this method of evaluation, S5 stated that the success of this sponsorship was not one that could be easily quantified in dollar terms, '*it comes down to something you can't measure in dollar terms, it's basically a public relations exercise*' (S5).

E5 stated that he conducted informal evaluations of the triathlon sponsorships, by way of verbal communication with sponsors in the weeks following the event. However, E5 did not identify which issues were discussed within these communications. It was stated that these informal evaluations were conducted with the intention of securing each sponsors' support for the following year's triathlon. E5 also mentioned that no formal feedback of sponsorship success was provided to sponsors, however '*we write an article in the* [local newspaper] *for them and give all the sponsors a mention in that*'.

In summary, both the sponsor and the event organisers undertook some evaluation of this sponsorship, with varying degrees of formality. Both parties undertook an evaluation partly for the purpose of making the process of sponsorship renewal for the following year somewhat easier. S5's positive attitude towards conducting this evaluation was reflected in this comment: '*I don't have to but did anyway for my own benefit*'. Meanwhile, E5 possessed a far more casual attitude towards evaluation.

How the Sponsorship was Initiated

E5 explained that this sponsorship came into place as a result of a request from the athletics club (who organises the triathlon) to the credit union in 1995. S5 was unable to provide a comprehensive insight into why the credit union accepted the athletics club's request for sponsorship, owing to the fact he was not employed by the credit union at that time. However, S5 surmised that '*we probably saw it as an opportunity to foster an event that had the potential to become something rather large and an important event on the calendar each year which it has become. We've continued to support it and promote it*'.

In describing the level of formality involved with this sponsorship relationship, E5 described it as '*a handshake agreement*' with the credit union. Additionally, he described the triathlon's relationships with all of its sponsors as '*very informal*'.

To summarise, this sponsorship came to fruition via a formal request from the event organisers to the credit union, and has evolved to become a very informal, but mutually satisfying arrangement.

4.3 Chapter Summary

Chapter Four has presented the results obtained from qualitative interviews conducted with SME owner/managers and managers of regional sport tourism events in Northern New South Wales. Chapter Five now discusses the significance of these results to the literature presented in Chapter Two, pertaining to SME sponsorship of regional sport tourism events. Additionally, Chapter Five brings the literature and results of this study together to propose a process model of the cycle of SME sponsorship of regional sport tourism events.

CHAPTER FIVE

DISCUSSION

5.1 Introduction

This chapter provides a discussion of the results of this study into SME sponsorship agreements with regional sport tourism events. Sections 5.2 through 5.6 discuss the results of this research utilising the five research objectives (refer Section 1.3) as topics of discussion. Section 5.7 then proposes a process model of SME sponsorship of regional sport tourism events that emerged from the findings of this research and from the literature presented in Chapter Two.

5.2 Sponsor & Event Manager Perceptions of Sponsorship

The literature review found that numerous sponsorship researchers felt that sponsorship was dissimilar to philanthropy and was no longer viewed in this manner by those who engage in sponsorship today (Copeland et al., 1996; Head, 1988; Irwin & Asimakopoulos, 1992). Instead, sponsorship was seen as an exchange relationship in which two parties exchange resources of value to gain mutual benefit (McCarville & Copeland, 1994).

This study has shown that three of the five SMEs investigated defined sponsorship primarily as providing a cause with support, in the form of cash or in-kind products or services in exchange for some recognition of the contribution, which may result in increased awareness of the business. Table 5.1 summarises the definitions provided by the participants of this study. The two remaining businesses saw sponsorship strictly as philanthropy as they stated that they expected no return whatsoever on their sponsorship investment. Despite claims by the previously cited authors who felt that sponsorship is no longer viewed as philanthropy, this study has demonstrated that some SMEs do in fact still engage in sponsorship for philanthropic purposes.

One sponsor who defined sponsorship as consisting of mutual benefit to both parties was S2. It should be noted that case number two was by far the most expensive sponsorship of all the cases in this research. The fact that this business manager defined sponsorship in this manner may be attributed to the substantial sponsorship investment made by the registered club to the Masters Games. It is only natural that this business would expect a significant return for contributing such a considerable amount of money.

S1 and S4 stated that they did not engage in sponsoring a great deal of causes or events. This point was interesting in that both these sponsors defined sponsorship explicitly as philanthropy. Therefore, a question may be raised in future research asking whether SMEs that have a low degree of involvement in sponsorship perceive sponsorship to be philanthropy, as opposed to businesses that have a high degree of involvement.

Table 5.1: Definitions of sponsorship provided by research participants.

Case Number	Event Manager	Sponsor
1	'Showing your support for a particular event or sport by lending your name to that event and being prepared to pay for the privilege of lending your name, having your name on that event'	'Business charity'
2	'An agreement with a mutual benefit to both. But the benefit's definitely ours. We hold the cards but you don't be blasé about it because you want them to come back'	'An amount of money or in-kind service that we give to an organisation and in return they give us recognition'
3	'Somebody that comes to you and gives you cash or product to run an event for a club or organisation'	'Sponsorship is putting something back into the community that gives us so much, but in doing that you're also achieving awareness of your brand, whichever it whether it be real estate or a bottleshop or whatever...sponsorship is about putting something back into the community that services you on a daily basis...but we're also trying to seek awareness out of that as well'
4	'Giving money to assist a promotion, you don't get as much out of it as you put into it'	'Giving something to an event, we don't expect much out of it at the end of the day regardless of what it is'
5	'A necessary thing...it gives people access to prizes they normally wouldn't get'	'Providing support to an event or organisation that would otherwise struggle without that support...obviously there has to be some sort of benefit [to the sponsor] as far as promotion goes'

E5 stated that many of the sponsors of his triathlon provide sponsorship to the event each year *'because they don't like to say no'*. This comment was reflected in Mack's (1999) finding that 80% of small businesses sponsored the same events on a continuous basis. Similarly, Slack and Bentz (1996) found that small businesses felt that refusing a sponsorship request had the potential to damage a business' reputation through negative word of-mouth publicity. A future research question could investigate why regular sponsorship of events by the same small businesses becomes a 'norm' within such enterprises.

Four of the five event managers interviewed defined sponsorship as a one-sided relationship, with their event being the major beneficiary of the agreement. In describing these definitions as 'one-sided', the researcher meant that these definitions only encapsulated one side of the relationship, i.e. they did not define sponsorship as an exchange relationship, in which both parties exchange resources for mutual benefit. Crompton (1997) felt that the terms 'sponsorship' and 'donation' were used interchangeably and were seen as synonymous. It could therefore be argued that this research has substantiated Crompton's claim in the context of regional sport tourism event managers.

Of the five event managers interviewed for this research, three were unpaid volunteers (E3, E4 and E5). All three of these volunteer event managers defined sponsorship as a business donation, whilst only one professional event manager defined sponsorship as an exchange relationship. However, the professional event manager who did not define sponsorship as an exchange relationship (E1) mentioned throughout the interview that the turf club saw it as paramount that sponsors receive benefits proportionate to the value of their sponsorship contribution, which indicated that he did acknowledge the importance of exchange for mutual benefit, *'it's a balance for us between so that we are getting enough sponsorship money coming in one end while giving them enough benefits or perceived benefits is probably the better term, on the other side of it so they will back from year to year'* (E1).

The fact that volunteer event managers did not define sponsorship as an exchange relationship could be attributed to their lack of formal training and knowledge of sponsorship management. All three volunteers were self-employed in industries outside of sport management: one was a builder, one owned a bicycle store, and one owned a video rental business. It may be expected that such volunteers would not possess an intricate knowledge of managing sponsorships. It is therefore understandable that they would view sponsorship in such a manner. However, persons responsible for managing event sponsorships should be aware of the fact that SMEs do expect some benefits or return in exchange for their contribution, and should make some effort to facilitate a return for their sponsors.

The first objective of this study was to 'identify sponsors' and event managers' perceptions as to what constitutes sponsorship'. This study has shown that event managers and sponsors of regional sport tourism events generally did not share concurrent views of what constitutes 'sponsorship'. Sponsors demonstrated a perception of sponsorship which involved a contribution that yields some form of benefit in return, while event managers (particularly volunteer event managers), leaned towards a one-sided perception of sponsorship with the event being the major beneficiary. This research has also shown that some of the SMEs interviewed viewed sponsorship in a purely philanthropic practice.

5.3 Reasons why Small and Medium Businesses Provided Sponsorship to Regional Sport Tourism Events

The literature review established that SMEs engage in sponsorship primarily to give back to the community and for company image/goodwill purposes (Mack, 1999). The literature review also showed that small businesses sponsored regional sport tourism events to build and reinforce name recognition, to demonstrate good corporate citizenship, because sponsorship was considered to be a good advertising vehicle (Mount & Niro, 1995), to show corporate social responsibility and to enhance business image (Slack & Bentz, 1996).

This research identified a total of ten reasons why SMEs provided sponsorship to their respective regional sport tourism event. Table 5.2 summarises these reasons.

Table 5.2 Reasons cited by SMEs for sponsoring regional sport tourism events.

Reason	Number of Times Cited
Give back to community	4
Obtain media exposure/publicity	3
Increase awareness of business	2
Increase sales	2
Attract visitors to host town	2
Enhance image in community	1
Encourage participation in sport	1
External forces (government legislation)	1
To leverage business	1
Personal contact	1

It should be noted that the reasons identified in Table 5.2 were not ranked in order of importance by the respondents. The researcher assumed that the number of times each reason was cited throughout the course of the interviews may be indicative of the level of importance of each reason. Thus for the purpose of this section, this indicator of importance shall form the basis of the following discussion.

The most frequently cited reasons for sponsoring regional sport tourism events were to 'give back to the community' and to 'obtain media exposure/publicity'. This finding reflected those of Mount and Niro (1995) who conducted a study similar to this research in Canada. These researchers found that 'good corporate citizenship' (which can be likened to 'giving back to the community') was the most frequently cited reason for SMEs to sponsor regional sport tourism events. The findings of this research were also concurrent with Slack and Bentz (1996), who found that 'corporate social responsibility' was the most prevalent rationale by small businesses to sponsor regional sports events.

Given the relative concurrence of these three studies, a conclusion may be drawn that SMEs provide sponsorship to regional sport tourism events primarily for community-orientated purposes, as opposed to bottom-line driven objectives. Strength is added to this conclusion by the comment made by Abratt et al. (1987), who found local event sponsorships were undertaken by small businesses primarily due to an awareness of their social responsibility to their respective community. Additionally, Parker (1991) stated that businesses who engage in sponsorship for the purpose of being viewed as a good corporate citizen or to give back to the community often realise benefits in terms of philanthropy. Parker's view further substantiates a link between responses such as 'give back to the community' with philanthropy.

Reasons identified for SMEs sponsoring regional sport tourism events by this research that were not pointed out in previous similar studies were:

- To attract visitors to the host town;
- To encourage sport; and
- Due to personal contacts within the event organising body.

Sponsors S3 and S5 sponsored their respective events partly to facilitate the attraction of visitors from outside the host community. The fact that these businesses did this demonstrated that some SMEs were aware of the benefits to a community of hosting sports events outlined by Delpy (1998), such as economic benefits and smoothing out of demand for services. In fact, S3 (a real estate agent) was acutely aware of the direct benefits that could be accrued by his business through renting holiday accommodation to triathlon competitors, or perhaps in the very best case scenario, possibly sell a property to a competitor who took a liking to the triathlon's host community, *'I've only got to sell one house and I've covered my sponsorship of the triathlon for three or four years'* explained S3.

S5 (a community credit union) wished to achieve both philanthropic and bottom-line oriented objectives by attracting visitors to its community through the triathlon. The philanthropic objective was evident in the credit union's desire to assist a community group run an event in the small community, as S5 explained, *'it's nice to think that an organisation like ourselves can help a small group like that to achieve a recognised event'*. By facilitating the attraction of visitors to the town to compete in or watch the triathlon, the credit union also felt that it was contributing to its own bottom-line by gaining exposure to an audience outside of the local community, *'it just brings us to the focus of those people because one day they we might be there* [open a branch in a visitor's home town] *or one day they might move up here, so that brings us to their attention'* (S5).

When compared to large businesses sponsoring large-scale sport tourism events, differences were found to exist in the reasons why SMEs and large businesses sponsored sport tourism events. The most comparable study of this nature was that of Carter and Wilkinson (2000), who investigated the reasons motivating large businesses to provide sponsorship to the Sydney 2000 Olympic Games. These researchers found the following reasons (listed in order of importance) to be the drivers behind why such businesses sponsored this sporting mega-event:

1. Increase employee morale;

2. Showcasing a product or product line;

3. Reach specific audiences;

4. Enhance community image;

5. Increase brand awareness; and

6. Increase profits (Carter & Wilkinson, 2000, p. 177).

When compared with the ten reasons for SMEs to sponsor a regional sport tourism event identified by this research (refer Table 5.2), there was considerable difference. A desire to give back to the community (which arguably was a philanthropic objective) was the most frequently cited objective by SMEs in this study, compared with Carter and Wilkinson's (2000) finding of 'increasing employee morale' as large businesses' most important objective in sport tourism event sponsorship. It is arguable that sponsors' desire to 'increase employee morale' could be a strategy designed to increase productivity, which could result in increased profits (an objective which rated as number six in Carter and Wilkinson's findings). It should also be noted that only one of Carter and Wilkinson's findings was not directly linked to the bottom-line, which was to 'enhance community image'. Brown's (2000) findings also strongly suggested that large businesses sponsored sport tourism events for bottom-line oriented purposes. This lends further strength to an argument that a distinction exists between SMEs and large businesses in the reasons they sponsor sport tourism events.

Consequently, this researcher suggests that the primary difference in the reasons why SMEs sponsor regional sport tourism events in comparison to large businesses sponsoring large events, was that SMEs did so for community orientated (possibly philanthropic) purposes, as opposed to large businesses sponsoring sport tourism events for bottom-line oriented reasons.

This study has not authoritatively defined which were the most important reasons for SMEs to sponsor regional sport tourism events. Further inquiry is required. This researcher suggests that future research could take all the reasons identified in this study, along with those identified by Mount and Niro (1995) and Slack and Bentz (1996), and quantitatively rank them over a more representative sample which could be inferred to a wider population.

In summary, the second objective of this research was 'to identify the reasons why small and medium businesses provide sponsorship to regional sport tourism events'. This study identified ten reasons why SMEs provided sponsorship to regional sport tourism events. The findings were concurrent with similar research conducted by Mount and Niro (1995) and Slack and Betz (1996), and added further strength to the argument that SMEs provide sponsorship to regional sport tourism events primarily to benefit their respective communities as opposed to achieving bottom-line objectives. It was also found that some sponsors were aware of the financial and social benefits to a community resulting from hosting a sport tourism event, and that one sponsor was instrumental in conceptualising sport tourism events. Finally, this study identified a difference in the reasons why SMEs sponsor sport tourism events, as opposed to large businesses. SMEs did so for community-oriented purposes (some of which were arguably philanthropic), whilst previous studies showed that large businesses did so to satisfy bottom-line oriented objectives.

5.4 Leveraging Practices in Small and Medium Business Sponsorships of Regional Sport Tourism Events

In reviewing the literature pertaining to best practice in event sponsorship management, it was established that many researchers advocated the practice of *leveraging* a sponsorship in order for a sponsor to obtain the maximum possible return on its sponsorship investment (Abratt & Grobler, 1989; Arthur et al., 1998; Pope & Voges, 1994). Engaging in a sponsorship agreement without leveraging was viewed to be ineffective in generating any significant return for a sponsor (Sleight, 1989).

Table 5.3 provides a summary of the leveraging practices utilised by the participants in this research. It was found that there was a general lack of awareness by both event managers and sponsors of the need to leverage a sponsorship if a sponsor was to receive any significant return on investment. This study also revealed that some sponsors were in ideal positions to leverage business from their sponsorship but failed to do so, while some businesses leveraged their sponsorship without being aware of it. Professional event managers were found to be more proactive in encouraging their sponsors to leverage, as opposed to their volunteer counterparts. These findings are discussed in detail throughout this section.

Table 5.3: Summary of leveraging practices by research participants.

Case Number	Sponsor	Event Manager
1	Did not leverage.	Encouraged leveraging by sponsors and provided advice to facilitate leveraging.
2	Leveraged indirectly by: - Distributing bistro vouchers - Distributing bumper stickers - Distributing a CD featuring and explaining all the club's features - Requiring the Masters Games to hold all its major functions at the club.	Assisted in facilitating leveraging activities by sponsors if requested to do so.
3	Leveraged indirectly by: - Providing contact information on triathlon entry form that encouraged competitors to contact the sponsor for their accommodation needs.	Did not encourage sponsors to leverage and did not provide sponsors with information as to how they might capitalise on their sponsorship.
4	Did not leverage	Did not encourage sponsors to leverage and did not provide sponsors with information as to how they might capitalise on their sponsorship.
5	Leveraged indirectly by: - Placing promotional material and triathlon entry forms in local branch.	Provided minor leveraging advice to some sponsors.

A lack of awareness by event managers and sponsors of the need to leverage sponsorships was apparent in the findings of this research. This was evident by the fact that two sponsors did not leverage at all, while another two made attempts at leveraging which arguably, were ineffective. Interestingly, the two sponsors who did not leverage also defined sponsorship purely as an altruistic practice (refer Section 5.2), thereby further substantiating this researcher's claim that some SMEs engage in sponsorship for philanthropic reasons. Only one event manager adamantly stated that he encouraged effective leveraging practices, whilst two maintained casual and uninformed approaches to providing leveraging advice to their sponsors. The remaining two event managers did not encourage leveraging at all. However, these two event managers (E3 and E4) were volunteers, which suggests a lack of awareness of the importance of leveraging amongst volunteer event managers.

The sponsors of cases one (car dealership) and three (real estate agency) were in ideal situations to leverage business through their respective sponsorships but either failed to leverage at all, or failed to leverage effectively. In sponsoring the horse racing carnival, S1 was presented with an on-site audience of approximately 9,000 people, most residing within the business' local community. S1 stated that no attempt was made to leverage the sponsorship. However, if promotions such as an on-site display of vehicles, distribution of catalogues or promotional material to the crowd, or conducting a sales promotion of some kind had been executed, the car dealership may have been able to sow the seeds for a sale or at the very least, gain an increase in community awareness of the business and knowledge of the product it sells.

Similarly, S3 made only a minor attempt to leverage business from its sponsorship of the triathlon by encouraging visiting competitors to source their accommodation through the real estate agency. S3 stated that selling property in the host town was an objective of the sponsorship. Therefore the real estate agency could have done well to at least distribute property catalogues or similar promotional material to the triathlon competitors in their registration kits.

Three of the five sponsors did conduct some form of leveraging activity. However, these sponsors leveraged their sponsorship 'indirectly'. The researcher noted that these sponsors, when asked if they conducted any promotions associated with their sponsorship that were designed to enhance return on investment, stated that they did not.

However, throughout the course of the interviews, these sponsors gave evidence that they did attempt to leverage their sponsorship, albeit without being aware they were doing so. It should be emphasised that the researcher did not ask the interviewees 'if they leveraged their sponsorship', which eliminated the chance of the respondent being caught out unaware of the terminology. For example, S2 (registered club) was adamant that the club did not conduct any promotions associated with the Masters Games sponsorship, however, the following quote emerged later on during the interview which suggested otherwise:

> 'With all their pre-registration satchels, we put as much information in as we can – we're allowed to put anything in there. We put membership forms, bistro vouchers to encourage them to come back and use the bistro, we put little bumper stickers in so they can go away and put them on their cars and things like that. We also had a little CD made up that showed

the facilities in the club. If they're not local [the competitors] *they could show their friends and we would hopefully get a spin-off that way'* (S2).

As is clear from this quote, the registered club made a practical attempt to leverage their sponsorship of the Masters Games by distributing promotional material to Games competitors. In addition to distributing promotional material to competitors, the registered club also leveraged significant amounts of business from the sponsorship by insisting that all major functions of the Masters Games were held in the club's function rooms. As a result, three functions were held at the club which attracted between 2,500 and 4,000 people to the club each time.

Of all sponsors interviewed during the course of this research, S2 made the most definitive attempt to leverage business back from its sponsorship investment of a sport tourism event. However, it must be reiterated that this was the most expensive sponsorship of all the case studies, being a cash contribution in the vicinity of AU$20,000. Therefore, it would be expected that a comprehensive leveraging strategy would be implemented to ensure the sponsor received a reasonable return on this considerable investment.

Crompton (1993) stated that event managers should assist sponsors to achieve a return on their sponsorship investment. This study found that the two professional event managers did provide advice to their sponsors as to how they might capitalise on their investment, albeit with differing levels of exuberance. E1 vigorously encouraged his sponsors to leverage, as he was eager to foster sponsor satisfaction and thereby facilitate the process of sponsorship renewal for the following year. E2 stated that he was happy to provide leveraging advice and facilitate any leveraging activities, but would only do so upon request from a sponsor, *'we don't tell them how to do that, if they wanted to, we'd probably say yes we'll help you... but it's certainly our responsibility to help them'* (E2). The fact that these professional event managers provided leveraging advice to their sponsors may be attributed to training in sponsorship practices (for example, during tertiary studies) that these people may have undertaken, or possibly an accrued awareness through experience of their responsibility to ensure sponsor satisfaction if that sponsor is to lend support to future events.

In contrast, E3, E4 and E5 were volunteer event managers. Two volunteer event managers stated that they did not encourage leveraging by sponsors, nor did they provide any advice as to how a sponsor may capitalise on their investment. The remaining event manager (E5) stated that he provided some minor advice to one sponsor of the triathlon, *'the café wasn't going to be open when the triathlon was on, so we told them that the triathlon is going to be on at this time, and they opened those hours to cater for it'*. However, this advice can be considered casual and only vaguely related to leveraging practices as discussed in the literature (refer Section 2.11).

The findings of this research demonstrated that volunteer event managers possessed a limited awareness of their obligation to assist sponsors obtain a return on investment from sponsoring their event. These findings echoed the view of Crompton (1993) who felt that event organisers frequently disregarded the fact that other communications tools must be utilised in order for a sponsor to obtain maximum benefit from its sponsorship. The opinion of Brooks (1994) was also reflected in these findings; Brooks stated that the organisers of minor sports events have been slow to recognise the value of corporate promotional spending, and this study has substantiated Brooks' statement in a regional sport tourism event context. An argument may be posed that organisers of small events take sponsors for granted and perceive them purely as a source of event income and nothing more, which may form a future research question. Interestingly, the following quote from one event manager (who shall not be identified) alluded to this proposed argument:

> 'I'd rather they just gave me the money actually. But their organisation obviously expects them to deliver...generosity is not a motivating factor anymore, it plays a part and no doubt we get sponsors who tend to be interested in sport, therefore it tickles their fancy but we still have to deliver a return'.

.Mount and Niro (1995) found that small businesses employed a range of techniques in leveraging their sponsorship of regional sport tourism events. Such techniques included in-store advertising, in-store displays, word-of-mouth promotion and not leveraging at all. The techniques used by the SMEs who did attempt to leverage their sponsorship identified by this study were:

- Distribution of promotional material to event participants;
- Hosting event functions in-house;
- Business logo and contact information printed on event entry form; and
- In-store display (e.g. poster in window, event entry forms at counter).

The responses 'in-store display' and 'did not attempt to leverage' identified by this research were also identified by Mount and Niro (1995). The leveraging techniques identified by this research have shown that even when an SME does engage in leveraging, the techniques employed were not overly sophisticated, and may not have been overly effective in attracting business back to a sponsor.

Parker (1991) noted that techniques commonly employed by large businesses to leverage sponsorships included:

- Production of merchandise;

- Advertising;
- Promotions;
- Competitions; and
- Point-of-sale material.

From the techniques identified by Parker (1991), it is apparent that techniques employed by SMEs identified in this study were different to those used by large businesses. The techniques identified by Parker would be considerably more expensive to employ, which could perhaps explain why SMEs opted for less sophisticated and possibly less expensive means of leveraging their sponsorships. It may also be that SMEs were less willing to spend money on leveraging activities owing to their smaller marketing budgets, compared to those of large businesses.

'To explore if and how leveraging is conducted within small and medium business/regional sport tourism event sponsorships' was the third objective of this study. This section has shown that event managers and sponsors did not place a great deal of importance on sponsorship leveraging, except in instances where a sponsor contributed a substantial amount of monetary support. It was established that professional event managers possessed a greater awareness of the importance of sponsorship leveraging and appropriate techniques to facilitate the process. Finally, leveraging techniques employed by SMEs identified in this study differed from those used by large businesses. SMEs tended to use less sophisticated and less expensive methods than large businesses to leverage their sponsorships.

5.5 Evaluation of Small and Medium Business Sponsorships of Regional Sport Tourism Events

The literature review found that many businesses who engaged in sponsorship insisted upon quantifying the effectiveness of their sponsorship investment (Kuzma et al., 1993) Arthur et al. (1998) advocated the practice of sponsors implementing a set of SMART objectives (refer Section 2.12) to facilitate the evaluation process. The literature also stated that no one definitive process of sponsorship evaluation exists, and that the concept of sponsorship evaluation was still evolving. Conjecture existed as to which party was responsible for conducting an evaluation, however Copeland et al. (1996) and Geldard and Sinclair (1996) implied that the sponsored party was responsible.

Table 5.4 provides a summary of findings relevant to this discussion topic. This research found that either the sponsor or event manager in all but one case study carried out some form of sponsorship evaluation. Many evaluative techniques employed by the research participants were informal and of a non-systematic nature. These findings are now discussed in detail. From the limited available literature, no key differences were found in the methods used by SMEs and those used by large businesses in evaluating sponsorship effectiveness.

Some form of evaluation was carried out in all cases except case number four. In cases two, three and five, both the sponsor and event manager conducted an evaluation of the success of the sponsorship. These findings confirm that evaluation did occur within these SME sponsorships of regional sport tourism events.

Table 5.4: Summary of research findings pertaining to sponsorship evaluation.

Case No.	Did the Sponsor Evaluate?	Did the Event Evaluate?	Did the Sponsor have Objectives in Place?	Did the Sponsor Expect a Return?
1	No	Yes	No	No
2	Yes	Yes	Yes	Yes
3	Yes	Yes	Yes	Yes
4	No	No	No	No
5	Yes	Yes	Yes	Yes

In conducting sponsorship evaluations, a limited number of evaluative techniques employed by sponsors and event managers were identified. Table 5.5 summarises the evaluative techniques identified during the course of this research. 'Casual conversation' was a commonly cited evaluation technique, whereby the sponsor and event manager met and discussed positive and negative aspects of the sponsorship with the aim of renewing the sponsorship for the following year and to manage it in an improved manner. Every event manager who conducted an evaluation of their sponsorship utilised casual conversation with sponsors as an evaluative technique.

The sponsors of cases two and three were the only businesses to conduct an evaluation of their sponsorship using an evaluative technique that focused on the bottom-line. S2 performed the most sophisticated evaluation of all the sponsors interviewed during this research. In a similar form of cost-benefit analysis described by Meenaghan (1991), S2 compared the increase in the club's trading figures during the week of the Masters Games against the dollar amount of sponsorship given to the event in order to determine if the sponsorship had an impact on the club's bottom-line. Conducting this more sophisticated method of evaluation by S2 could be justified by the large amount of cash sponsorship contributed to the Masters Games, and that the impact of the sponsorship on the club's bottom-line would have needed to be reported to the club's executive.

Table 5.5: Summary of evaluative techniques used by sponsors and events identified by this research.

Case No.	Evaluative Techniques: Sponsor	Evaluative Techniques: Events	Did Event provide Sponsor with Written Feedback?
1	None	- Casual conversation - Period of time taken for sponsor to pay sponsorship fee	No
2	- Cost-benefit analysis - Press coverage analysis	- Quantitative survey - Casual conversation	Yes
3	Sales impact assessment	Casual Conversation	No
4	None	None	No
5	Press coverage analysis	Casual conversation	No

S3, a real estate agent, was the other business to conduct a bottom-line oriented evaluation. In this instance, S3 evaluated the success of the sponsorship based upon the number of his agency's holiday accommodation properties that were occupied during the weekend of the triathlon. As all of S3's properties were occupied, plus the fact that the business had managed to rent out another twenty holiday properties on behalf of other real estate agents in the town, S3 declared the sponsorship of the triathlon as having a high short-term impact upon his business. This form of evaluation was unsophisticated, but because S3 was able to satisfy himself that the sponsorship had a direct impact on his business confirmed in his mind that he had achieved his objective in sponsoring the triathlon.

It may be possible that SMEs were unwilling to spend additional funds on comprehensively evaluating the effectiveness of their sponsorships and were content to use unsophisticated methods of evaluation, so long as they could satisfy themselves that their sponsorship had a positive impact upon their business.

Research by Mount and Niro (1995) identified the following methods used by small businesses to evaluate the effectiveness of their sponsorship of regional sport tourism events:

- Feedback from customers;
- Increase in store traffic;
- Increase in sales revenue;
- Based on return on investment; and
- Did not evaluate at all.

The findings of this study differed slightly from those of Mount and Niro (1995) in that this study identified 'analysis of press coverage' as an evaluative technique used by SMEs, whereas Mount and Niro did not. The cost-benefit analysis used by the registered club in case number two can be paralleled to 'based on return on investment' and 'increase in sales revenue' from Mount and Niro's results, as S2 was assessing both of these factors in its evaluation of the Masters Games sponsorship. Nevertheless, this research has added to the body of knowledge pertaining to SME sponsorship evaluation techniques in that such businesses frequently look to the amount of press coverage generated by their sponsorships as an evaluative measure.

A theme that also arose from this research was a feeling amongst sponsors that sponsorship effectiveness was difficult to measure and hard to quantify in dollar terms, as the following quotes demonstrate:

> *'It comes down to something you can't measure in dollar terms, it's basically a public relations exercise'* (S5).
>
> *'I was once told by a very smart man in advertising that if you can't measure the success of your advertising, then don't...it's very difficult'* (S1).
>
> *'It's a bit hard to measure'* (S2).
>
> *'We just don't know how we could do that [conduct a formal evaluation]'* (S3).

Abratt and Grobler (1989) found that many of the businesses they studied did evaluate their sponsorships but did not have a formal system of evaluation in place. These researchers also found that four of the twenty-eight businesses surveyed did not have any measurable objectives in place to evaluate their sponsorships against. Abratt and Grobler's findings were reflected in this research in that none of the sponsors interviewed had any specific, measurable, attainable, relevant and trackable (SMART) objectives in place to guide their sponsorships and to provide a benchmark to evaluate against, which was a practice advocated by Abratt and Grobler (1989) and Arthur et al. (1998). Some sponsors had objectives in place that they wished to achieve through sponsoring their respective sport tourism event, however such objectives were often vague and did not facilitate the process of evaluation. S3 for example (real estate agent) stated that the objective he wished to achieve through sponsoring the triathlon was simply *'awareness'* of his business. This objective was neither specific nor measurable, therefore when evaluating his sponsorship, S3 could not have concluded if this objective was achieved or not.

The two sponsors (S1 and S4) who did not evaluate their sponsorships were the two businesses identified in Section 5.2 who viewed sponsorship as philanthropy. Such sponsors also did not make any attempt to leverage their sponsorships. These factors assist in confirming that these two businesses engaged in their sponsorships purely for philanthropic reasons and were content to simply be involved in a community-based event. S1 stated that *'it's just nice to be involved with something along those lines'* as the central reason why the car dealership is involved with sponsoring the horse racing carnival.

The evaluative tool of choice amongst event managers was casual conversation with sponsors in the aftermath of the event. In many instances, event managers met with sponsors in the weeks following an event either through an informal meeting, or at a sponsors' 'thank you' function (such as a breakfast or similar) during which they discussed the positive and negative aspects of the sponsorship. One event manager described this conversational evaluation as *'a post-event function with the sponsors which is usually just a breakfast or something and we ask them very candid questions…happy, sad, good, bad, happy, why, how come?'* (E2).

This study detected a preference for a casual, qualitative approach to evaluation over written surveys by organisers of regional sport tourism events. One event manager commented that meeting with a sponsor and discussing the success of the sponsorship was more effective than posting out written, quantitative surveys. He stated that *'you tend to get the good oil from the verbal process'* (E2). It should be noted that E2 utilised both a written survey and casual conversation when evaluating the effectiveness of the sponsorship he was involved in. He felt that it was difficult to obtain high response levels from sponsor surveys and that sponsors tended to only fill written surveys out when they were dissatisfied with the benefits they received.

Another event manager expressed a disliking of written surveys to evaluate sponsor satisfaction. He cited being fearful of sponsors demanding benefits that his event was incapable of delivering, which may threaten the viability of gaining sponsorship for his event in the future, *'we're scared of the answers we're going to get. We might start getting demands that we can't meet or are too difficult to do on the day, because it's such a hectic day'* (E1).

In a general sense, the event managers interviewed during the course of this research exhibited a low level of knowledge of sponsorship evaluation and appropriate methods for conducting an evaluation. Of the five event managers interviewed, only one appeared competent in his ability to evaluate sponsorship effectiveness (who was a professional event manager). The issue of sponsorship evaluation remains to be somewhat blurred within the literature, particularly regarding the selection of appropriate evaluation methods and level of complexity involved in an evaluation. Crompton (2004) described the literature addressing sponsorship evaluation as 'underdeveloped' (p. 268). It is therefore understandable that organisers of regional sport tourism events (particularly volunteer event managers) would not possess an intricate knowledge of the process of sponsorship evaluation. Arthur et al. (1998) stated that the process and rigour involved in an individual sponsorship evaluation was highly dependent upon the value of a sponsorship, and that sponsorships of higher value will attract an evaluation process much more rigorous and complex than those involving less expenditure. Consequently, the informal and unsophisticated methods of evaluation used by event managers in this study may be attributed to a reflection of the monetary value of the sponsorships investigated, many of which were relatively inexpensive.

Table 5.5 also illustrated that only one of the five events provided its sponsors with any form of written feedback pertaining to the effectiveness of sponsorship of a respective event. The event which did provide feedback was case number two (Masters Games). This was the most expensive sponsorship investigated, with a value of approximately AU$20,000, and was organised by a professional event organising body. These factors provide some rationalisation as to why feedback was provided to sponsors of this event. It is also possible that the event managers may have been attempting to facilitate the renewal of sponsorships for next time the event is to be held.

The remaining four events did not provide any written feedback pertaining to sponsorship effectiveness to their sponsors. According to Geldard and Sinclair (1996), event managers should provide sponsors who have contributed up to AU$1,000 to an event with at least two reports. One report should be in the form of a periodical newsletter in the lead-up to the event, which serves to add value to sponsoring the property. The second should be in the form of a generic report distributed to all sponsors which outlines participant/spectator numbers, television coverage and the like, and should include an individualised section for each sponsor detailing the sponsor's involvement in and benefits received from sponsoring the event. The fact that none of these events attempted to provide feedback to their sponsors was of some concern. Such lack of reporting may create a perception of lack of involvement in an event amongst sponsors. This may compromise future sponsorships, which could threaten revenue sources for these events and thereby compromise their long-term viability. Sport tourism events at the regional level should make some effort to provide written feedback to their sponsors, even if it is a token gesture to make the sponsors feel valued and encourage ongoing support for the event.

There was a distinct lack of previous studies examining the leveraging techniques used by large businesses to evaluate the effectiveness of sport tourism event sponsorships. This meant that a comparison of this study's findings to those of large businesses was difficult. However, Crompton (2004) did identify through content analysis of sponsorship industry publications, five broad areas through which large businesses evaluated their sponsorships of sport events. These were:

1. Measuring media equivalencies;
2. Measuring impact on awareness;
3. Measuring impact on image;
4. Measuring impact on intent to purchase; and
5. Measuring impact on sales.

This research found that press coverage analysis, cost-benefit analysis and assessment of impact on sales were the evaluative tools used by those SMEs who did evaluate. Some of these findings were similar to those of Crompton (2004) in that 'assessment of impact on sales' could be seen as an interchangeable term with Crompton's 'measuring impact on sales', and 'press coverage analysis' is exchangeable with Crompton's 'measuring media equivalencies'. Additionally, the cost-benefit analysis used by S2 could arguably be categorised as a measurement of impact on sales. Therefore, this research was relatively concurrent with the findings of Crompton (2004). No major differences existed between the methods used by small, medium and large businesses in evaluating the effectiveness of sport tourism event sponsorships. Debatably, the only difference between small, medium and large businesses in this respect may have been the level of rigour, complexity and expense allocated to evaluating such sponsorships. Again, Arthur et al's (1998) statement must be reiterated that the level of rigour and complexity engaged in evaluating a sponsorship will be a function of a sponsorship's dollar value.

Research objective four of this study was to 'explore if and how event managers and sponsors evaluated the effectiveness of their sponsorship relationship'. Section 5.5 discussed the occurrence and practices of sponsorship evaluation by the SMEs and regional sport tourism events that took part in this study. It was established that evaluation of sponsorship effectiveness was common amongst these sponsorship agreements, however the rigour and complexity employed for such evaluations was concurrent with the monetary value of each respective sponsorship, which in many cases was low. A distinct lack of sponsorship evaluation reporting to sponsors existed amongst the events studied. Little difference was found in the methods used by SMEs to evaluate their sponsorships and those used by large businesses, however, the comparison made in this discussion was hampered by a lack of previous research to compare this against.

5.6 The Initiation of Sponsorship Agreements between Small and Medium Businesses and Regional Sport Tourism Events

The limited literature relating to this point of discussion established that personal contacts between a business owner/manager and with an individual on the organising committee of an event played a pivotal role in initiating sponsorship agreements between SMEs and regional sport tourism events (Slack & Bentz, 1996). Meanwhile, Mount and Niro (1995) found that an overwhelming majority of SMEs became involved in sponsoring regional sport tourism events as a result of being approached by the event organisers.

Table 5.6 provides a summary of the sponsorships studied were initiated and their level of formality. Two of the five sponsorships (cases two and five) were initiated through a request from event organisers to the respective businesses for sponsorship. This outcome represented less than 50% of the sample, while research by Mount and Niro (1995) found that 88% of their business respondents had been approached by organisers of sport tourism events requesting sponsorship.

Table 5.6: Summary of how sponsorship agreements were initiated and level of formality involved.

Case No.	How Agreement Started	Level of Formality
1	Personal contact	Handshake agreement
2	Request from event organisers	Contract signed by both parties
3	Request from sponsor to sporting organisation	Handshake agreement
4	Personal contact	Handshake agreement
5	Request from event organisers	Handshake agreement

Four of the five sponsorships were described by either the sponsor or event manager as 'handshake agreements'. In describing a handshake agreement, this tended to mean that no legal documents or contracts were in place to dictate the responsibilities and contribution to the agreement by the involved parties. 'Handshake' sponsorship agreements were essentially agreements whereby the responsibilities and contributions of the sponsor and property were agreed upon and sealed by a handshake as opposed to having a legally binding contract drawn up and signed by each party. Such agreements could also be likened to 'gentlemen's agreements', which Krebs (1985) defined as an 'agreement binding by honour but not valid in law' (p. 214).

A further two sponsorships (Cases one and four) arose as a result of 'personal contacts'. A personal contact in this context generally involved an individual who was part of the organising committee for an event personally knowing someone who either owned or managed a business that would be suitable to approach for sponsorship of the event. For example, case number four involved a bus company supplying a number of buses to ferry ocean swim competitors from the registration venue to the race start area. This sponsorship was initiated by a member of the ocean swim classic organising committee who knew the manager of the bus company on a personal basis. This was evidenced by the following quote from S4, *'we just did it, probably more because we knew Ken'*.

Sponsorship agreements between SMEs and smaller sport events were also discussed by Slack and Bentz (1996), who found that a number of their respondents stated that, 'owner/manager preferences and/or personal contacts were highly significant factors in affecting which teams or events were sponsored' (p. 178). It could be argued that in cases where personal contacts played a significant role in an SME's decision to sponsor a sport tourism event, that *trustworthiness* of the event manager was highly sought after by potential sponsors. In describing this argument, it may be that SMEs wanted to be confident in an event manager's ability to conduct a successful and reputable event; that sponsorship of an event will yield positive benefits to the business as opposed to possible negative publicity gained through association with an unsuccessful or controversial event. If a business owner already has a personal connection with an event's organisers, then the risk a business takes in sponsoring that event may be lowered owing to the business manager's existing knowledge of the event manager's reputation and capabilities. Such an argument has been mentioned previously in the study by Mount and Niro (1995), in which one of their respondents commented on the importance of 'being able to trust the event organisers' (p. 174) being an influential factor in the decision to sponsor or not.

This discussion point has potential for future research. A question could be posed asking whether SMEs are more likely to provide sponsorship to events in which the business owner/manager personally knows an individual on the organising committee, as opposed to events in which the owner/manager does not know anyone on the organising committee. Further, a question could ask whether trustworthiness of the event organisers is a more influential factor in an SME's decision to sponsor a regional sport tourism event, than the benefits package on offer to them.

Literature discussing how sponsorships encompassing large event and large businesses were initiated could not be located. This meant that a comparison of how regional sport tourism event sponsorships were initiated with SMEs as opposed to the large event/business context was not possible.

The fifth and final objective of this study was to 'examine how sponsorship agreements between small and medium businesses were initiated with regional sport tourism events'. Section 5.6 has shown that the sponsorships studied in this research were initiated through one of three ways: via personal networks; through a request to a business from event organisers; or through a request from a business to event organisers. It was also established that these sponsorships were informal agreements sealed by a handshake between a sponsor and an event manager, similar to a gentlemen's agreement. Personal contacts of persons involved in event organising committees were though to have played a role in an SME's decision to sponsor an event or not. Further research is required to substantiate this claim.

5.7 Process Model of Regional Sport Tourism Event Sponsorship by Small and Medium Businesses

This section proposes and discusses a process model of regional sport tourism event sponsorship by SMEs (Figure 5.1). Though not an initial objective of the present study, during compilation of the discussion chapter, it became apparent that a diagrammatical model could be constructed to illustrate the process of SME sponsorship of regional sport tourism events that was emerging from the literature and the outcomes of this research. A discussion of the proposed model is provided in this section.

The model is encased in a broken rectangle which represents a regional community. This makes the model exclusive to communities distant from international ports of entry to a country (Centre for Regional Tourism Research, 2001). The rectangle is presented in a broken manner to acknowledge the theory of an open system, whereby an organisation (a region in this case) 'must interact with the environment to survive…it must continuously change and adapt to the environment' (Daft, 1992, p. 9). Environmental factors that could influence a region in this regard might include the availability of persons skilled in event management, similar events being held in other locations at concurrent times, or even the economic climate (for example high fuel prices may deter people from travelling long distances to an event).

Within the model are eight numbered boxes which represent sequential steps in the sponsorship cycle, which are followed in a clockwise direction. Box number one represents a community's desire to accrue benefits associated with hosting an event, which include increased income resulting from visitor spending, employment, smoothing out of troughs in demand for services (Dowell, 1999), and intangible benefits such as increased community spirit and cooperation (Walo et al., 1996).

Regional communities often lack the financial resources to construct specific infrastructure to host one-off sports events. However, according to Dowell (1999) sport tourism events hosted by regional communities can often make use of existing infrastructure to host events and be of low cost to the community. Thus, hosting a sport tourism event may provide an ideal way for a community to accrue some or all of the benefits previously mentioned.

REGIONAL COMMUNITY

1. REGIONAL COMMUNITY
SEEKS:
- Injection of capital
- To reduce seasonality
- To generate employment

At low cost – Can be achieved through a small sport tourism event

POSSIBLE RENEWAL OF SPONSORSHIPS FOR FOLLOWING YEAR

8. EVALUATION OF SPONSORSHIPS
Event organisers and sponsors evaluate through:
- Informal conversation
- Analysis of press coverage
- Assessment of impact on sales

2. EVENT CONCEPTUALIZATION
- Facilities audit conducted
- Community sporting groups consulted
- Appropriate event identified
- Organising committee formed

7. EVENT CONCLUDED
- Local economy strengthened by visitor spending
- Seeds sown for repeat visitation
- Event receives good/bad publicity in media
- Stakeholder evaluation of event impacts

Potential for Mutual Benefit

3. EVENT REQUIRES INITIAL REVENUE TO BE VIABLE
POSSIBLE REVENUE SOURCES:
- Local government grant
- Sponsorship from local small and medium enterprises (SMEs)

APPROACHES LOCAL SMEs FOR SPONSORSHIP

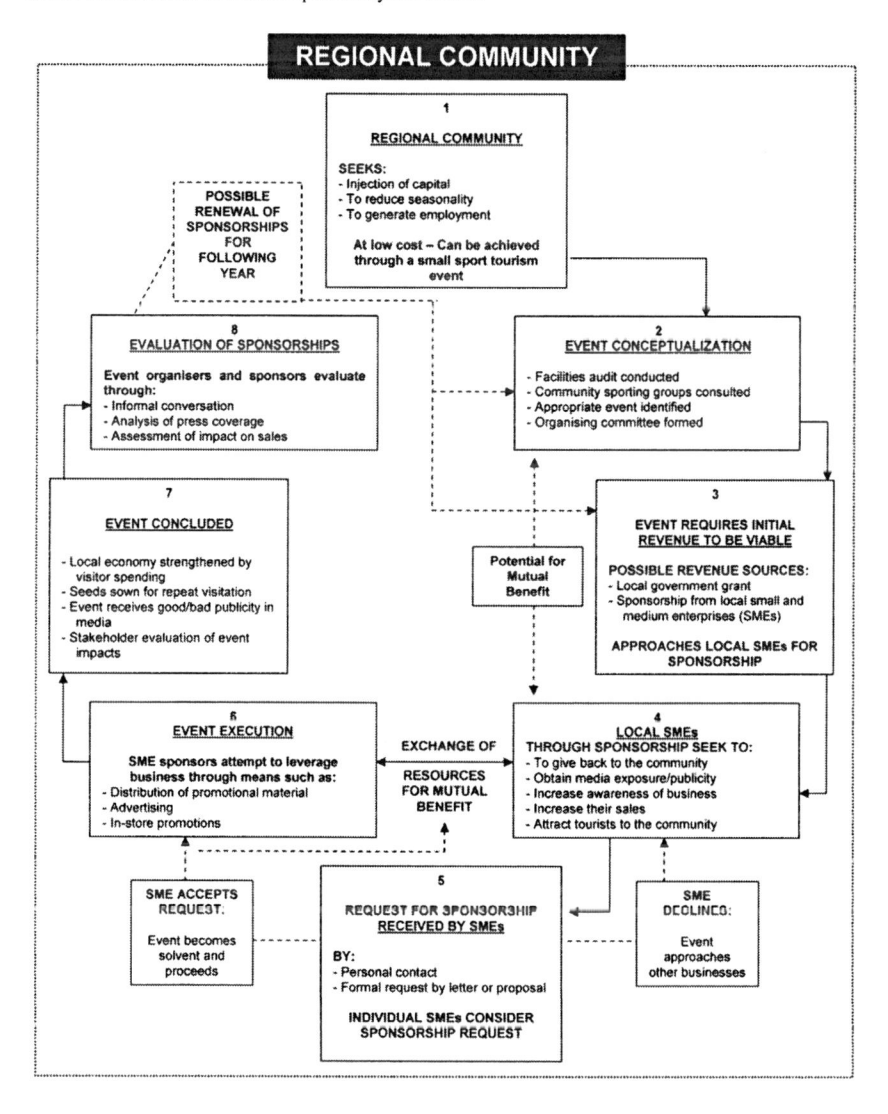

6. EVENT EXECUTION
SME sponsors attempt to leverage business through means such as:
- Distribution of promotional material
- Advertising
- In-store promotions

EXCHANGE OF RESOURCES FOR MUTUAL BENEFIT

4. LOCAL SMEs
THROUGH SPONSORSHIP SEEK TO:
- To give back to the community
- Obtain media exposure/publicity
- Increase awareness of business
- Increase their sales
- Attract tourists to the community

SME ACCEPTS REQUEST.
Event becomes solvent and proceeds

5. REQUEST FOR SPONSORSHIP RECEIVED BY SMEs
BY:
- Personal contact
- Formal request by letter or proposal

INDIVIDUAL SMEs CONSIDER SPONSORSHIP REQUEST

SME DECLINES:
Event approaches other businesses

Figure 5.1: Process model of regional sport tourism event sponsorship by SMEs (source: original for this study).

Box number two represents the event conceptualisation phase of the sponsorship cycle. It may be during this phase that a community's desire for the benefits associated with event tourism have been recognised. Therefore, the aim of this phase would be to identify an appropriate event that is within the community's capacity to conduct. Not only does a community need sporting infrastructure to host a sport tourism event, it also requires sufficient backup infrastructure such as accommodation and restaurants to cater for the anticipated number of people converging on the host community. Consequently it is suggested that a facilities audit be conducted, a process advocated by the Federal Department of Industry Science and Resources (2000). Once the scope of a community's capacity to host an event has been identified, consultation with sporting organisations can identify an appropriate event that can be staged and an organising committee formed.

Box number three represents the need for an event to obtain initial funds to become viable. Allen et al. (2002) identified eight sources of income available to an event, however it is debatable that only three of those sources may be available prior to an event taking place. They were broadcast rights, government grants, and sponsorship. It could be argued that regional events would not realistically be able to sell off broadcast rights due to their low appeal to television audiences. Consequently, this eliminates broadcast rights as a source of revenue, leaving government grants and sponsorship as the two sources of start-up revenue for a regional event. The literature stated that on average, 43% of any given event's budget comprised of sponsorship revenue (IEG, 1992a), therefore it may be surmised that organisers of events will look to sponsorship funds over government grants to obtain initial revenue. Given that large corporations tend to be located in major cities, it is likely that organisers of regional sport tourism events will approach either small or medium size businesses for sponsorship.

Box number four represents SMEs in a regional community. This research, along with previous studies by Mount and Niro (1995) and Slack and Bentz (1996) established that SMEs sponsored regional sport tourism events primarily to achieve the five objectives identified in this box. Broken lines or boxes in this model depict possible linkages, dependent upon a decision being made. For example, boxes two and four are linked with a broken arrow, depicting a possible relationship between a conceptualised event and an SME, should a business agree to sponsor an event. This possibility exists due to the event's need for start-up revenue and SMEs desire to achieve the five objectives listed in box number four.

Box number five depicts the request for sponsorship phase by the event to an individual SME. This research along with the work of Mount and Niro (1995) and Slack and Bentz (1996), found that many regional sport tourism event sponsorships were initiated through personal contacts of event organisers with SME owners or managers, or via a formal request from event organisers to an SME, hence the presence of these options in box number five. Linked by broken arrows to either side of box number five are two option boxes. If an SME accepts the sponsorship request, the event becomes financially solvent and may proceed, and as such the model continues to be followed clockwise. Should an SME reject the request, the model is followed anti-clockwise back to box number four where an event manager may select an alternate business to request sponsorship from.

If start-up revenue cannot be sourced, it is reasonable to suspect that an event may not be able to proceed. Box number six represents the event execution phase, where an event has been made financially solvent by either one or a combination of cash contributions from SME sponsors and was able to proceed. The 'SME accepts request' option box is linked by a broken arrow to a solid arrow depicting the actual exchange of resources resulting in mutual benefit for the event and sponsor, as outlined in the definition of sponsorship by Sandler and Shani (1989), adopted to guide this research. Also encased in box number six are the leveraging practices of SMEs as identified by this research and those identified by Mount and Niro (1995), which SMEs use to capitalise on their sponsorship investment.

Box number seven represents the phase of the sponsorship cycle whereby an event has been staged and the community may have begun to accrue the desired benefits of event tourism identified in box number one. The event may be scrutinised by stakeholders such as organisers, sponsors, local government, local businesses and residents as to whether the event was successful, and the impacts it has had on the community are identified, whether they be positive or negative.

Finally, box number eight represents the evaluation phase of the SME sponsorships which provided initial solvency to the event. This research along with Mount and Niro (1995) identified three primary ways in which SMEs and event organisers evaluated the sponsorships of regional sport tourism events, which included informal conversation, analysis of press coverage, and assessment of impact on sales. An emerging theme from this research showed that event managers occasionally use these informal sponsorship evaluations to facilitate the renewal of sponsorships if the event is to be held again in the future. Thus, an option box presented in a broken line is present which recognises a possible attempt at sponsorship renewal. Broken arrows provide possible links from the renewal option box to boxes two and three. In doing so, provision is made (through the possible link to box number three) for renewing the sponsorship cycle for the next time the event is staged. Alternatively, by linking to box number two, scope is provided for the community to reconceptualise the event in the case of the original event being unsuccessful.

5.8 Chapter Summary

Chapter Five has discussed the findings of this research that were presented in Chapter Four. Additionally, this chapter has proposed a process model of regional sport tourism event sponsorship by SMEs. The proposed model may benefit persons involved in the management of SME sponsorships of regional sport tourism events, and also those studying sport tourism at tertiary level, by providing an illustration of the sponsorship cycle in this context. Chapter Six now provides the conclusion to this work and outlines the management implications arising from this research into the sponsorship of regional sport tourism events by SMEs.

CHAPTER SIX

CONCLUSION AND IMPLICATIONS

6.1 Summary of the Study

Chapter Five discussed the findings of this research in relation to the literature presented in chapter two. Additionally, a variety of original concepts were proposed as well as a process model of SME sponsorship of regional sport tourism events. Chapter Six concludes this work by providing a summary of the research and presenting the managerial implications arising from this study, the limiting factors surrounding this research, and recommended areas for future research.

This research set out to achieve five specific objectives which were designed to elicit an overall picture of SME sponsorship of regional sport tourism events. The objectives of this research pertained to sponsor and event manager's perception of the term 'sponsorship'; the reasons driving SMEs to sponsor regional sport tourism events; operational functions of sponsorship agreements; leveraging and evaluation; and finally, how sponsorship agreements between SMEs and regional sport tourism events were initiated.

It was found that the event managers and SME sponsors studied during the course of this research shared differing views of what constitutes 'sponsorship'. Many of the SME sponsors viewed sponsorship as a mutually beneficial exchange of resources between two parties, which incited a supposition that these businesses desired some sort of return on their sponsorship investment. Meanwhile, event managers tended to exhibit a perception that viewed sponsorship as a one-sided relationship in which their event was the major beneficiary and was not expected to offer a great deal to the sponsor in return. This was particularly the case with volunteer event managers, however this perception was attributed to a lack of formal training in the management of sponsorships. Professional event managers demonstrated a superior understanding of the need to reciprocate benefits to their sponsors.

The reasons identified by this study as to why SMEs sponsored regional sport tourism events tended to relate to a desire by SMEs to support their local community, as opposed to achieving bottom-line orientated objectives. The findings in this regard were relatively concurrent with previous research conducted by Mount and Niro (1995) and Slack and Bentz (1996) who found that SMEs sponsored sports events primarily for community-based reasons. It was also found that some SMEs sponsored regional sport tourism events purely for philanthropic purposes because they did not expect anything in return for their contribution. Differences were detected between SMEs and large businesses in the reasons why they sponsored sport tourism events. As previously mentioned, SMEs sponsored primarily to support their local community, whilst large businesses sought to achieve bottom-line objectives such as increasing sales, launching new product lines and gaining large amounts of media exposure.

This research explored if and how two operational functions of sponsorship occurred within sponsorship agreements between SMEs and regional sport tourism events: leveraging and evaluation. It was found that the SME sponsor conducted some form of leveraging within three of the five cases studied, while three of the event managers interviewed encouraged leveraging by their sponsors, albeit with varying levels of enthusiasm. The results demonstrated a low degree of awareness amongst sponsors and event managers of the need to leverage a sponsorship if the sponsor was to exploit the full potential of a sponsorship, except in instances where a sponsor had contributed a substantial amount of cash sponsorship. The leveraging techniques employed by SMEs in this study were less sophisticated and therefore less expensive to execute as opposed to those used by large businesses to leverage their event sponsorships. Finally, professional event managers tended to possess a more intricate awareness of the need for, and appropriate methods of leveraging sponsorships than their volunteer counterparts.

The 'underdeveloped' (Crompton, 2004, p. 268) body of knowledge pertaining to sponsorship evaluation was reflected in the findings of this research. The sponsor or event organisers in all but one case study conducted some form of sponsorship evaluation, however a lack of knowledge as to how to evaluate the sponsorships was evident amongst the participants. The most common method of sponsorship evaluation involved casual conversation between event organisers and sponsors, during which candid questions were exchanged between each party regarding the positive and negative aspects of the sponsorships in addition to potential areas of improvement. Only one event reported that it provided any form of written feedback to its sponsors pertaining to sponsorship effectiveness, which highlighted a lack of reporting to sponsors on the part of the events studied. Similar to leveraging, the evaluative techniques employed by SMEs tended to be unsophisticated and inexpensive to execute when compared to those used by large businesses, however this comparison was hampered by a lack of previous research to compare against.

Finally, this study examined how sponsorship agreements between regional sport tourism events and SMEs were initiated. It was found that such sponsorships were initiated through one of three ways: via personal networks; through a request to a business from event organisers; or through a request from a business to event organisers. It was also found that all but one of the sponsorships studied were bound by 'gentlemen's agreements' whereby the responsibilities of each party were agreed upon and sealed by a handshake as opposed to a legally binding contract.

6.2 Management Implications arising from this Research

A number of implications for the management of sponsorships of regional sport tourism events by SMEs have arisen from the outcomes of this research. They are discussed throughout this section.

More often than not, managers of regional sport tourism events will deal with SMEs when attempting to acquire sponsorship funds to stage their events. This study, along with others such as Mount and Niro (1995) and Slack and Bentz (1996) has demonstrated that differences exist in the way sponsorships are managed according to the size and scope of a) the event, and b) the sponsor involved. Large businesses sponsoring large events tended to employ sophisticated and complex processes of leveraging and evaluation. In contrast, SME sponsorships of regional sport tourism events were less formal by nature with SMEs looking to achieve different objectives to large businesses through sponsoring such events, which was reflected in the manner such sponsorships are managed. Consequently, there is no one generic process for managing a sponsorship; the process will vary according to the size of the business, the size of the event, and the value of the sponsorship involved.

Therefore, a key implication arising from this research is that a distinction must be made between SMEs and large business sponsorships in two situations. The first being when compiling educational material for persons studying event management, the second being whilst conducting research into the sponsorship of events.

This study has shown that some event managers tended to view sponsorship as being interchangeable with the term 'donation', which is incorrect. Sponsorship by definition infers that a return is expected by the sponsor (Sandler & Shani, 1989). It can be argued that within many regional communities, organisers of sport tourism events may only have a limited pool of potential businesses from which to source sponsorship funds. Consequently, it is vital that event managers are proficient in managing sponsorships, because if a point of dissatisfaction amongst sponsors in a small community is reached, event managers may struggle to acquire necessary revenue to sustain their events. Therefore, another implication stemming from this research is that event managers of regional sport tourism events should make an attempt to become more adept in managing sponsorships. This researcher suggests the publication of a handbook designed to educate managers of regional sport tourism events (particularly volunteers), outlining the nature of sponsorship along with practical guidelines for operational functions such as leveraging and evaluation. Responsibility for publishing such a handbook should fall on organisations such as government departments or tourism bodies whose functions include facilitating sport tourism as a means of economic development in regional areas.

This research also has practical implications for event managers when attempting to solicit sponsorship from SMEs. When compiling sponsorship proposals, managers of regional sport tourism events could do well to emphasise that providing sponsorship to their event would be an ideal way of giving back to, and supporting their local community. In doing this however, an onus would be placed on event organisers to conduct successful, controversy-free events which benefit the community. Event managers may also benefit from looking to businesses in which they have personal contacts for sponsorship. However, further research is required to confirm if a relationship does exist between personal contacts and an increased probability of sponsorship being provided.

Event managers may also enhance their chances of obtaining sponsorship if they design their event to be 'leverage friendly', and create opportunities for sponsors to leverage business back through their doors and facilitate a return on investment for their sponsors.

It was found that all but one event in this study provided its sponsors with some form of written feedback regarding sponsorship effectiveness. The literature stated that it is best practice for event managers to provide their sponsors with a post-event précis sponsorship report if a property is to place itself in the best position for renewal of a sponsorship (Copeland et al., 1996; Geldard & Sinclair, 1996). Therefore, organisers of regional sport tourism events need to adopt this practice, even if it is merely a token gesture to offer a sponsor some extra tangible value and making them feel involved in and valued by the event.

Some SMEs examined in this research did not make any attempt to leverage their sponsorship. The literature assertively stated that purchasing a sponsorship opportunity is ineffective as a stand-alone technique of generating a return on investment (Arthur et al., 1998; Meenaghan, 1991; Sleight, 1989). Therefore, if an SME does desire a return on investment, when considering a proposition to sponsor a regional sport tourism event it should ask itself a) is there scope to leverage business from the sponsorship? And b) if appropriate methods of leveraging are available within the business' resources to effectively capitalise on the proposed sponsorship? Failure to consider these questions may result in an SME's sponsorship of an event being inadvertently transformed into a donation, with no real benefit to the business.

6.3 Contribution to Knowledge

This research has contributed to the current bodies of knowledge regarding sport tourism, corporate sponsorship, and the management of special events by:

1. Addressing a gap in the sport tourism literature by examining the management of sponsorships by regional sport tourism events;

2. Expanding the event management literature by proposing an illustrative model of the sponsorship cycle involving SMEs and regional sport tourism events; and

3. Adding to the corporate sponsorship literature by identifying practical implications for organisers of regional sport tourism events attempting to solicit sponsorship from SMEs.

6.4 Limitations of the Research

Due to the qualitative case study strategy employed to undertake this study, the findings of this research cannot be extrapolated to a wider population (Jennings, 2001). They are exclusive to the events and the SMEs who participated in this study. Furthermore, because of the epistemological interaction between the researcher and the participants, if another person conducted the interviews, it is likely that responses would be somewhat different to those obtained by this researcher.

The outcomes and implications arising from this research are limited to SMEs and regional sport tourism events. The managerial implications may not be transferable to other types of events or business sizes.

This study was also limited geographically to the research area defined in Section 3.6. It was necessary to geographically limit the study to the defined area, due to the relatively short timeframe imposed to conduct the research and the limited resources available to the researcher to conduct a study of broader geographical scope.

6.5 Recommended Areas for Future Research

This study has demonstrated that the sponsorship agreements between SMEs and regional sport tourism events remain somewhat of a misunderstood phenomenon in academia. It is important that research continues into the sponsorships of regional sport tourism events to continue to build a body of knowledge that can then be dispensed to persons involved in managing such sponsorships. Future research conducted into event sponsorship should clearly distinguish between small, medium and large businesses. It is important to make this distinction, as studies such as this have demonstrated that differences exist in the manner in which businesses of different sizes manage their sponsorships.

A number of areas for future research have arisen from this particular study, which are outlined in this next section. Where appropriate, a reference is included to the relevant section of the discussion chapter from which many future research questions arose.

SMEs that did not engage in a lot of sponsorship tended to perceive sponsorship as philanthropy (refer Section 5.2). A future study may ask whether a relationship exists between SMEs level of involvement in sponsorship (whether they frequently or infrequently engage in sponsorship) and their perception of sponsorship (philanthropy or means of achieving bottom-line objectives).

Some SMEs tended to exhibit a pattern of sponsoring the same events year after year, regardless of whether the sponsorship was generating a return on investment or not (refer Section 5.2). Another interesting study could investigate why sponsorship of the same events becomes a 'norm' within SMEs.

This study, along with Mount and Niro (1995) and Slack and Bentz (1996) have identified a battery of reasons cited by SMEs as to why they sponsor regional sport tourism events (refer Section 5.3). Collectively, these reasons could form the basis of a quantitative instrument which could be administered to a larger, more representative sample. The outcomes of such a study could rank the responses and be inferred to a wider population of SMEs. A more conclusive comparison may then be made against the reasons why large businesses sponsor sport tourism events.

This research showed that volunteer event managers possessed a limited awareness of their obligation to assist sponsors to obtain a return on investment from sponsoring their events (refer Section 5.4). This led to an argument being proposed by the researcher that organisers of regional sport tourism events take sponsors for granted and perceive them purely as a source of event income and nothing more. A future study could investigate if there is any substance to this argument.

In some instances, personal contacts between SME owners and event organisers were influential in a sponsorship agreement being initiated (refer Section 5.6). Future research may ask whether SMEs are more likely to provide sponsorship to events in which the SME owner/manager personally knows an individual on the organising committee, as opposed to events in which the SME owner/manager does not have personal contacts on the organising committee.

Owing to some SMEs sponsoring events in which they had personal contacts with, a supposition was made that SMEs see trustworthiness of the event organiser(s) as an influential factor in their decision to sponsor an event or not (refer Section 5.6). The final suggestion for future research arising from the present study is a study examining whether trustworthiness of the event organiser(s) is an influential factor in an SMEs decision to sponsor a regional sport tourism event or not.

REFERENCES

Abratt, R., Clayton, B., & Pitt, L. (1987). Corporate objectives in sport sponsorship. *International Journal of Advertising, 6*, 299-311.

Abratt, R., & Grobler, P. (1989). The evaluation of sports sponsorship. *International Journal of Advertising, 8*(4), 351-362.

Allen, J., O'Toole, W., McDonnell, I., & Harris, R. (2002). *Festival and special event management* (2nd ed.). Milton, QLD: J. Wiley & Sons.

Amis, J., Pant, N., & Slack, T. (1997). Achieving a sustainable competitive advantage: A resource-based view of sport sponsorship. *Journal of Sport Management, 11*(1), 80-96.

Amis, J., Slack, T., & Berrett, T. (1999). Sport sponsorship as distinctive competence. *European Journal of Marketing, 33*(3/4), 250-272.

Arthur, D. (1999). *The decision-making process of corporate sport sponsorship in Australia*. Unpublished PhD thesis, Southern Cross University, Lismore, Australia.

Arthur, D., Scott, D., & Woods, T. (1997). A conceptual model of the corporate decision-making process of sport sponsorship acquisition. *Journal of Sport Management, 11*(3), 223-233.

Arthur, D., Scott, D., Woods, T., & Booker, R. (1998). Sport sponsorship should...A process model for the effective implementation and management of sport sponsorship programmes. *Sport Marketing Quarterly, 7*(4), 49-60.

Australian Bureau of Statistics. (1999). *Business sponsorship* (4144.0). Canberra.

Australian Bureau of Statistics. (2001). *Small business in Australia* (1321.0). Canberra.

Bennett, R. (1997). Corporate philanthropy in France, Germany and the UK: International comparisons of commercial orientation towards company giving in European nations. *International Marketing Review, 15*(6), 458-475.

Brooks, C. (1994). *Sports marketing: Competitive business strategies for sports*. Englewood Cliffs, NJ: Prentice Hall.

Brown, G. (2000). Emerging issues in Olympic sponsorship: Implications for host cities. *Sport Management Review, 3*, 71-92.

Brown, G. (2002). Taking the pulse of Olympic Sponsorship. *Event Management, 7*(3), 187-196.

Burgan, B., & Mules, T. (1992). Economic impact of sporting events. *Annals of Tourism Research, 19*(4), 700-710.

Carlsen, J. (2003). *Riding the wave of event sponsorship: Sponsorship objectives and awareness at the Margaret River Masters surfing event.* Proceedings of the CAUTHE 2003 Conference, Coffs Harbour, NSW, Australia.

Carter, L., & Wilkinson, I. (2000). *Reasons for sponsorship of the Sydney 2000 Olympic Games.* Proceedings of the ANZMAC 2000 Conference: Visionary Marketing for the 21st Century: Facing the Challenge, Gold Coast, QLD, Australia.

Centre for Regional Tourism Research. (2001). *Australian regional tourism handbook: Industry solutions 2001.* Lismore, NSW, Australia: Cooperative Research Centre for Sustainable Tourism.

Copeland, R., Frisby, W., & McCarville, R. (1996). Understanding the sport sponsorship process from a corporate perspective. *Journal of Sport Management, 10*(1), 33-48.

Corbett, J., & Lekush, J. (2003). NASCAR sponsorship: Putting your company in the driver's seat. *Journal of Integrated Communications, 2002-2003 issue*, 17-22.

Coughlan, D., & Mules, T. (2001). Sponsorship awareness and recognition at Canberra's Floriade Festival. *Event Management, 7*(1), 1-9.

Creswell, J. (1994). *Research design: Qualitative and quantitative approaches.* Thousand Oaks, CA: Sage.

Crompton, J. (1993). Understanding a business organization's approach to entering a sponsorship partnership. *Festival Management & Event Tourism, 1*(3), 98-109.

Crompton, J. (1994). Benefits and risks associated with sponsorship of major events. *Festival Management & Event Tourism, 2*(2), 65-74.

Crompton, J. (1995). Factors that have stimulated the growth of sponsorship of major events. *Festival Management & Event Tourism, 3*(2), 97-101.

Crompton, J. (1997). Partnering with business: What's in it for them? *Journal of Park & Recreation Administration, 15*(4), 38-60.

Crompton, J. (2004). Conceptualization and alternate operationalizations of the measurement of sponsorship effectiveness in sport. *Leisure Studies, 23*(3), 267-281.

Crowley, M. (1991). Prioritising the sponsorship audience. *European Journal of Marketing, 25*(11), 11-21.

Daft, R. (1992). *Organization theory and design* (4th ed.). St Paul, MN: West.

Daniels, M. (2004). Beyond input-output analysis: Using occupation-based modelling to estimate wages generated by a sport tourism event. *Journal of Travel Research, 43*(1), 75-82.

Daniels, M., & Norman, W. (2003). Estimating the economic impacts of seven regular sport tourism events. *Journal of Sport Tourism, 8*(4), 214-222.

Decker, J. (1991). Seven steps to sponsorship. *Parks and Recreation, 26*(12), 44-48

DeKnop, P. (1998). Sport tourism: A state of the art. *European Journal for Sport Management, 5*(2), 5-17.

Delpy, L. (1998). An overview of sport tourism: Building towards a dimensional framework. *Journal of Vacation Marketing, 4*(1), 23-36.

Delpy, L., Grabijas, M., & Stefanovich, A. (1998). Sport tourism and corporate sponsorship: A winning combination. *Journal of Vacation Marketing, 4*(1), 91-101.

Dowell, R. (1999). *Sports tourism: Something of substance or just another passing fad?* Proceedings of the Council for Australian University Tourism and Hospitality Education (CAUTHE) Conference, Adelaide, Australia.

Faulkner, B., Chalip, L., Brown, G., Jago, L., March, R., & Woodside, A. (2001). Monitoring the tourism impacts of the Sydney 2000 Olympics. *Event Management, 6*(4), 231-246.

Federal Department of Industry Science & Resources. (2000). *Towards a national sports tourism strategy (draft)*. Canberra.

Gardner, M., & Shuman, P. (1988). Sponsorships and small business. *Journal of Small Business Management, 26*(4), 44-52.

Geldard, E., & Sinclair, L. (1996). *The sponsorship manual*. Olinda, VIC, Australia: The Sponsorship Unit.

Getz, D. (1991). *Festivals, special events, and tourism*. New York: Van Nostrand Reinhold.

Getz, D. (1997). *Event management and event tourism*. New York: Cognizant Communications.

Getz, D., & Fairley, S. (2004). Media management at sport events for destination promotion: Case studies and concepts. *Event Management, 8*(3), 127-139.

Gibson, H. (1998). Sport tourism: A critical analysis of research. *Sport Management Review, 1*(1), 45-69.

Gibson, H., Attle, S., & Yiannakis, A. (1998). Segmenting the sport tourist market: A lifespan approach. *Journal of Vacation Marketing, 4*(1), 52-64.

Guba, E. (1990). *The paradigm dialogue*. Newberry Park, CA: Sage.

Hall, C. (1992). Adventure, sport and health. In C. Hall & B. Weiler (Eds.), *Special Interest Tourism*. London: Belhaven Press.

Head, V. (1988). *Successful sponsorship*. Cambridge, UK: Director Books.

Higham, J. (1999). Sport as an avenue of tourism development: An analysis of the positive and negative impacts of sport tourism. *Current Issues in Tourism, 2* (1), 82-90.

Hinch, T., & Higham, J. (2001). Sport tourism: A framework for research. *International Journal of Tourism Research, 3*(1), 45-58.

IEG. (1992a). Centrefold: Quantifying sponsorship. *IEG Sponsorship Report, 11* (22), 4-5.

IEG. (1992b). Coors shifts Keystone ties into high gear. *IEG Sponsorship Report, 11* (6), 6.

IEG. (1996). Slicing the pie. *IEG Sponsorship Report, 15*(23), 4.

IEG. (2003). Sponsorship spending to increase 8.7% in 2004. *IEG Sponsorship Report*, 22(24), 4.

International Olympic Committee. (2004). *Olympic Marketing Factfile 2004*, available at: http://www.olympic.org/common/asp/download_report.asp?file=en_report_344.pdf&id=344 -.

Irwin, R., & Asimakopoulos, M. (1992). An approach to the evaluation and selection of sport sponsorship proposals. *Sport Marketing Quarterly, 1*(2), 43-51.

Jago, L., & Shaw, R. (1998). Special events: A conceptual and definitional framework. *Festival Management & Event Tourism, 5*(1/2), 21-32.

Javalgi, R., Traylor, M., Gross, A., & Lampman, E. (1994). Awareness of sponsorship and corporate image: An empirical investigation. *Journal of Advertising, 23*(4), 47-58.

Jennings, G. (2001). *Tourism research*. Milton, QLD, Australia: J. Wiley & Sons.

Kinney, L., & McDaniel, S. (1996). Strategic Implications of attitude-toward-the-ad in leveraging event sponsorships. *Journal of Sport Management, 10*(3), 250-261.

Kolah, A. (2003). *Maximising the value of sponsorship (Abstract)*: Sport Business Associates. Available at: http://www.sportbusiness.com/reports/Value_of_Sponsorship.adp.

Kotler, P., Brown, L., Adam, S., & Armstrong, G. (2001). *Marketing*. Frenchs Forest, NSW, Australia: Prentice Hall.

Krebs, W. (1985). *The new Collins Australian compact English dictionary*. Sydney, Australia: W.M. Collins Sons & Co.

Kuzma, J., & Shanklin, W. (1994). Corporate sponsorship: A framework for analysis. In P. Graham (Ed.), *Sport Business, Operational and Theoretical Aspects*. Dubuque, IA: Brown and Benchmark.

Kuzma, J., Shanklin, W., & McCally, J. (1993). Number one principle for sporting events seeking corporate sponsors: Meet benefactor's objectives. *Sport Marketing Quarterly, 2*(3), 27-32.

Lee, M., Sandler, D., & Shani, D. (1997). Attitudinal constructs towards sponsorship: Scale development using three global sporting events. *International Marketing Review, 14*(3), 159-169.

Leiper, N. (1995). *Tourism management*. Melbourne, Australia: RMIT Press.

Lincoln, Y., & Guba, E. (1985). *Naturalistic inquiry*. Newbury Park, CA: Sage.

Long, P., & Perdue, R. (1990). The economic impact of rural festivals and special events: Assessing the spatial distributions of expenditures. *Journal of Travel Research, 28*(4), 10-14.

Mack, R. (1999). Event sponsorship: An exploratory study of small business objectives, practices, and perceptions. *Journal of Small Business Management, 37*(3), 25-30.

Marshall, C., & Rossman, G. (1999). *Designing qualitative research* (3rd ed.). Thousand Oaks, CA: Sage.

Marshall, D., & Cook, G. (1992). The corporate (sports) sponsor. *International Journal of Advertising, 11*(4), 307-324.

McCarville, R., & Copeland, R. (1994). Understanding sport sponsorship through exchange theory. *Journal of Sport Management, 8*(2), 102-114.

McDonald, C. (1991). Sponsorship and the image of the sponsor. *European Journal of Marketing, 25*(11), 31-38.

Meenaghan, T. (1991). The role of sponsorship in the marketing communications mix. *International Journal of Advertising, 10*(1), 35-47.

Meenaghan, T. (2001). Sponsorship and advertising: A comparison of consumer perceptions. *Psychology and Marketing, 18*(2), 191-215.

Meerabeau, E., Gillett, R., Kennedy, M., Adeoba, J., Byass, M., & Tabi, K. (1991). Sponsorship and the drinks industry in the 1990s. *European Journal of Marketing, 25*(11), 39-56.

Merriam, S. (1998). *Qualitative research and case study applications in education*. San Francisco: Jossey-Bass.

Miles, M., & Huberman, A. (1994) *Qualitative data analysis*. Thousand Oaks, CA: Sage.

Minichiello, V., Aroni, R., Timewell, E., & Alexander, L. (1995). *In-depth interviewing* (2nd ed.). Melbourne, Australia: Longman.

Molm, L. (1990). Structure, action, and outcomes: The dynamics of power in social exchange. *American Sociological Review, 55*(3), 427-447.

Morris, D., & Irwin, R. (1996). The data-driven approach to sponsorship acquisition. *Sport Marketing Quarterly, 5*(2), 7-10.

Mount, J., & Niro, B. (1995). Sponsorship: An empirical study of its application to local business in a small town setting. *Festival Management & Event Tourism, 2*(3/4), 167-175.

Mullin, B., Hardy, S., & Sutton, W. (1993). *Sport marketing*. Champaign, Il: Human Kinetics.

Murphy, P., & Carmichael, B. (1991). Assessing the tourism benefits of an open access sports tournament: The 1989 B.C. Winter Games. *Journal of Travel Research, 29*(3), 32-36.

Neuman, W. (2003). *Social research methods: Qualitative and quantitative approaches* (5th ed.). Boston: Allyn and Bacon.

Otker, T. (1988). Exploitation: The key to sponsorship success. *European Research,* May Edition, 77-86.

Parker, K. (1991). Sponsorship: The research contribution. *European Journal of Marketing, 25*(11), 22-30.

Parker, R. (2000). Small is not necessarily beautiful: An evaluation of policy support for small and medium-sized enterprises in Australia. *Australian Journal of Political Science, 35*(2), 239-253.

Patton, M. (2002). *Qualitative research and evaluation methods* (3rd ed.). Thousand Oaks, CA: Sage.

Pope, N., & Voges, K. (1994). Sponsorship evaluation: Does it match the motive and the mechanism. *Sport Marketing Quarterly, 3*(4), 37-45.

Pope, N., & Voges, K. (1997). An exploration of sponsorship awareness by product category and message location in televised sporting events. *Cyber Journal of Sport Marketing, 1*(1), 16-27.

Quinn, E. (1982) in Marshall, D., & Cook, G. (1992). The corporate (sports) sponsor. *International Journal of Advertising, 11*(4), 307-324.

Sandler, D., & Shani, D. (1989). Olympic sponsorship vs. ambush marketing: Who gets the gold? *Journal of Advertising Research,* August/September Edition, 9-14.

Sandler, D., & Shani, D. (1993). Sponsorship and the Olympic Games: The consumer perspective. *Sport Marketing Quarterly, 2*(3), 38-43.

Scott, D., & Suchard, H. (1992). Motivations for Australian expenditure on sponsorship - An analysis. *International Journal of Advertising, 11,* 325-332.

Skinner, B., & Rukavina, V. (2003). *Event sponsorship.* Hoboken, NJ: J. Wiley & Sons.

Slack, T., & Bentz, L. (1996). The involvement of small businesses in sport sponsorship. *Managing Leisure, 1*(3), 175-184.

Sleight, S. (1989). *Sponsorship: What it is and how to use it.* Berkshire, UK: McGraw-Hill.

Speed, R., & Thompson, P. (2000). Determinants of sports sponsorship response. *Journal of the Academy of Marketing Science, 28*(2), 226-238.

Standeven, J., & DeKnop, P. (1999). *Sport tourism.* Champaign, Il: Human Kinetics.

Stotlar, D. (1999). Sponsorship in North America: A survey of sport executives. *International Journal of Sports Marketing and Sponsorship, 1*(1), 87-100.

Stotlar, D. (2001). *Developing successful sport sponsorship plans.* Morgantown, WV: Fitness Information Technology.

Stotlar, D. (2004). Sponsorship evaluation: Moving from theory to practice. *Sport Marketing Quarterly, 13*(1), 61-64.

Suchard, H., & Scott, D. (1992). Sponsorship practices in Australia. *Management Research News, 15*(4), 18-27.

Sunshine, K., Backman, K., & Backman, S. (1995). An examination of sponsorship proposals in relation to corporate objectives. *Festival Management & Event Tourism, 2*(3/4), 159-166.

Turco, D. (1998). Fields of dreams: Sponsorship opportunities in sport tourism. *Visions in Leisure and Business, 17*(2), 13-17.

Turner, M. (2001). *Critical funds: Sponsorships in Australia and how to get them.* Ringwood, VIC, Australia: Penguin Books.

URS Finance and Economics. (2004). *Economic impact of the Rugby World Cup 2003 on the Australian economy - Post analysis.* A report commissioned by the Department of Industry, Tourism and Resources. Available at: http://www.ausport.gov.au/fulltext/2004/feddep/FinalEconomicImpactOfRWC2003.pdf.

Walo, M., Bull, A., & Breen, H. (1996). Achieving economic benefits at local events: A case study of a local sports event. *Festival Management & Event Tourism, 4*(1), 95-106.

World Travel and Tourism Council. (2005). *2005 Travel and tourism economic research (Executive Summary).* Available at: http://www.wttc.org/2005tsa/pdf/Executive_Summary_2005.pdf.

Yin, R. (2003). *Case study research: Design and methods* (3rd ed.). Thousand Oaks, CA: Sage.

Zauhar, J. (1996). Historical perspectives of sports tourism. *Journal of Sport Tourism, 3*(3), 7-181.

Appendix A

Interview Questions: Event Managers

1. How do you identify appropriate sponsors for your event and how do you approach them for sponsorship?

2. Can you describe some previous experiences with obtaining sponsorship for your event? (Name some)

3. If you had to define the term 'sponsorship', how would you define it?

4. What do you believe are the key characteristics of a successful sponsorship between a sponsor and an event?

5. Do you provide any advice or information to your sponsors as to how they may enhance the return on their sponsorship investments? If yes, can you describe the type of advice you provide?

6. Can you describe how you ascertain whether your sponsors are satisfied with the outcomes of providing sponsorship to your event?

7. Can you describe how you provide feedback to your sponsors with regard to their contribution to your event?

Appendix B

Interview Questions: Sponsors

1. How did the sponsorship relationship between your business and [name of event] start? And, how has it developed over time?

2. Can you tell me the reasons why you provide sponsorship to [name of event]?

3. If you had to define sponsorship, how would you define it?

4. How do you decide what events or causes to provide sponsorship to?

5. In sponsoring [name of event], can you describe the support you provide to this event?

6. Did your business invest any extra funds in promotional activities that were aimed at enhancing your return on this sponsorship? If yes, can you describe the activities you conducted in your sponsorship of [name of event]?

7. How do you evaluate the success of your sponsorship of [name of event]? [If yes] what techniques did you use in evaluating this sponsorship?

8. How important is sponsorship evaluation in maintaining the relationship with [name of event]?

VDM publishing **house ltd.**

Scientific Publishing House

offers

free of charge publication

of current academic research papers, Bachelor´s Theses, Master's Theses, Dissertations or Scientific Monographs

If you have written a thesis which satisfies high content as well as formal demands, and you are interested in a remunerated publication of your work, please send an e-mail with some initial information about yourself and your work to *info@vdm-publishing-house.com.*

Our editorial office will get in touch with you shortly.

VDM Publishing House Ltd.
Meldrum Court 17.
Beau Bassin
Mauritius
www.vdm-publishing-house.com